BEFORE
WE MET

To the onlie begetters

with much love

from

Tony and Marelle

January 2009

BEFORE WE MET

A MEMOIR BY

MARCELLE & ANTHONY QUINTON

STUYVESANT
NEW YORK

Published by Half Moon Press, Stuyvesant, New York.

Printed in the United States by Integrated Book Technologies, Troy, New York.

Library of Congress Control Number: 2008937587

ISBN: 978-0-615-25288-9

THIS BOOK IS FOR

SARAH, TOMMY,

JANE, GRACE, MARY KATE,

OLIVIA, ELLA,

RUPERT AND BENEDICT

WITH OUR LOVE.

MARCELLE

CHAPTER ONE
BERLIN

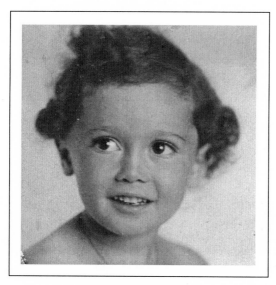

Marcelle: aged two

I entered the world a month late, after a difficult birth, on the 20th of May in the Jewish hospital in Wannsee, a suburb of Berlin. I was a great disappointment as my parents had wanted a boy and I was named Marcella. My parents had got married in Vienna in 1929. This was made necessary by my father's lack of 'papers' – that loose term referring to everything from permits to passports which, along with 'les devises' was the luggage of Europeans of that era. My father, the second of 11 children, was born Moshe Jossel Wengier (the surname means 'the Hungarian' in Polish) in what was then Russia (Poland after WW1) in the village of Mrodzeov. He crossed the border to Germany as a deserter from the army in 1917, never to return until he was deported there by the Nazis in 1938. My mother, the third of 6 children, was born

CHAPTER ONE: MARCELLE

Hedwig Leipziger in Upper Silesia. Their Polish passports were simplified: Moritz Wegier and Jadwiga Wegier. My father ran a specialized construction business (*Moritz Wegier Baugeschäft*) converting large houses into flats. My mother oversaw the book-keeping in the office near the Zoo at Monbijou Platz 1. We lived comfortably in Grunewald where once a year a large pile of sand was delivered for my sandpit, a present from Wilaszek who looked after building materials for my father.

Tony and I went to Berlin in 1990 and stayed at the Kempinski which I had heard of in hushed tones as a child. I walked up Wissmanstrasse to 11-11A, the red brick house, rather like those in North Oxford, still stood there; it was now an animal sanctuary. The garden seemed smaller. But the whole street had the same peaceful air of leafy suburb. Quite near was the Grunewald U Bahn Station, with the same thatched roof, from which the transport to the East was despatched in the forties.

The garden in Wissmanstrasse was very beautiful. Herr Dender looked after it and had very knobbly fingers, not long and slim like my father who, like all Poles, had beautiful hands. Part of the garden was reserved for the landlord, Herr Barrasch. He was a forbidding man in a suit, carrying a cane that he pointed upwards to count the cherries on his tree. That was the forbidden fruit in this particular Eden, and I ate thereof, and was revealed at the following day's counting. I was told it was stupid. There was also an aviary with small blue and yellow birds – quite different from the dark birds in the garden from which they had to be protected in their vast ornate cage. Indoors there was a winter garden with a small pool which was constantly filled from the mouth of a stone fish.

My father, having left his religion behind him with his *tefillin* when he left Poland, nevertheless presided over Friday evening and (knowing the Hagaddah by heart) Passover. After lunch on Sunday we went for a 'Verdauungsspaziergang' in the Grunewald (*nach dem Essen muss mann stehen oder tausend Schritte gehen*). We ate delicious meals prepared by our cook Margarethe, and I had a series of Fraüleins. In the summers we went to Holland and in the winters to St. Moritz or Davos for the 'Schielauffen'. When, at four I got my first pair of skis, they had to be made for me as nothing that small existed. Watching the tracks behind in the fresh powder snow is a thrilling and salutary experience: they could always have been closer (like parking a car, the space could always have been smaller when viewed from the kerb).

The gentle rhythm of life became more jolted by events outside. The advent of Hitler in 1933 had no effect immediately, nor did most people think he was going to last or that things would get worse. As the German schools were already out of bounds, my parents enrolled me, in 1935, in the American School in Berlin. But after a very short while, Dr. Ziemer, the Principal, told my parents that unfortunately he could no longer keep me (or any other Jewish children). He was a kindly man and later went to Ohio to run a radio station.

An English Miss was engaged to give some formality to my education. She insisted that a 'Löffel' was in fact a 'spoon' which I denied, and after much struggle agreed to compromise "kann mann auch sagen." Discouraged and fearful of the black Luftwaffe planes in the sky, she returned to England. In 1936 I was sent to a school in Celerina while my parents skied in nearby St. Moritz. There I was told stories about the Weihnachtsmann, who brought presents. But I held my own with stories of the Hannukah Man with a much longer beard who brought many more presents. I couldn't understand that food not eaten at midday would be served to you cold in the evening, when it was even less appetising. However, I was never sent back to find out.

It was wonderful when my Grandmother (Johannah Leipziger – born Beuthner) came to visit. She lived in Beuthen (now Byton) in upper Silesia, and loved to travel. She was widowed very early, in 1910 (my grandfather Isidor was an architect, specialising in building prisons). She came with a great load of presents. When I stayed with her, in 1937 I think, we went to the market together and she came home with a live carp wrapped in brown paper which was then left to swim about in the bathtub until it was time to be cooked. We went to Karlsbad where she took the waters every year. I had never drunk warm water before and ran around the various pumping stations sampling the water out of the tin cups. Omi retired to bed early with a hot water bottle, some paté and green pickles which she loved and knew didn't agree with her. She was very happy in Czechoslovakia and perished too soon in Theresienstadt in 1942.

Another very welcome visitor was my aunt Grete (Margarete, my mother's elder sister). She said she was very delicate and sat in a deckchair in the garden needing quiet, otherwise she would see little stars behind her eyes. I thought this might be quite agreeable and rubbed my eyes but never got to see the little stars. I visited her in Gleiwitz (now Gliwice) where she was the manageress of the largest department store, Karpe. I was allowed to go under the tables with a magnet to pick up the stray pins – dangerous and exciting work. Everything in Tante Grete's apartment was green. She even had a green bathtub and a green satin cover on her bed. In 1939 she managed to get a passage to Buenos Aires where she stayed until she came to New York after the war. She was overworked and underpaid in my Uncle Henry's office until she retired aged 75.

My uncle Hans Heinrich Leipziger, born January 1900, was the eldest. When in 1933, Jews were no longer permitted to work for non-Jews, he had to leave his position at a metal import and export business, moved to Luxembourg and set up on his own. In 1938, now Henry J. Leir, he and my aunt Erna moved permanently to New York. From there he orchestrated a worldwide business of importing metals with romantic names like fluorspar and molybdenum.

The restrictions on Jews did not affect us, but slowly slowly the daily routine changed. It was so gradual that no particular event stands out to be named: today we are repressed, today we have lost our freedom. The (unspoken) rules made one more circumspect – one moved to the other side of the street if Brownshirts appeared coming towards one. The parking or other fines for my father's dark blue Adler convertible became more hefty; the building permits more costly. But these were all inconveniences, outside the home. Meanwhile my father's business continued to prosper, as did most of Germany under Hitler.

A great boost was the Olympic Games in 1936. I had a brooch of the five intertwined rings in different coloured enamel and marvelled at its construction. The city was full of tourists and newspaper correspondents. Different languages were spoken in the streets by foreigners. Suddenly all was sweetness and light laughter and everyone was happy. The grownups talked of Jesse Owen: how could 'ein Neger' have won? And Leni Riefenstahl, was she a friend of the Führer's?

Around this time in 1936 it was decided that my mother and I should visit my father's family in Poland. It was wonderful for everyone. I had a new brown velvet skirt and matching coat, a pink silk blouse and a white satin one with ruffles down the front, also a pair of white glacé kid high shoes. We came with much luggage and pineapples. The family, headed by my great-grandfather, grandparents and 53 aunts, uncles and cousins, were all there. Their Yiddish easily translated into my German and I was happy to demonstrate my new skill of doing somersaults that they had not seen before. My grandparents' house had a shop in the front that my grandmother tended, where sacks of flour and beans got weighed and sold, and a room at the back where my grandfather and great-grandfather studied. There was a huge bed with a red velvet spread. My grandmother was lovely, she wore a scarf over her wig and was always fearful I might fall down. I was only fearful of the wooden box with sloping sides which was up a muddy path – lest I slide into the abyss with my new shoes – never to be seen again. On Friday the Shabbes Goy came to light the candles and after the meal they all took turns to play with me. Only my father's brother Kiwe, his wife and daughter Marysza survived Oswiecim and they came to New York after the war. They were quiet, blameless, religious, private, family-oriented people. They knew no life outside their village and no culture beyond the bible. Their world was just like countless similar *shtetls* that were destroyed and obliterated. Their murder by the Germans was abetted by the unfriendly local population. So, not only did these 53 cousins, aunts, uncles and grandparents perish never realising their potential or enriching the lives of others, but by systematically seeking out and murdering all the Jews, a whole way of life, culture and civilization was wiped out as well.

It became much, much worse in Germany once the Olympic celebrations came to an end. There was great commotion one day in early 1937. I was out with a maid to watch two fire engines dousing two buildings on either side of a synagogue that was engulfed in huge high yellow flames like a picture in a book. My parents decided that evening that from now I was to stay at home. Many synagogues burned down that day in official vandalism. Also hit were some shops on the Kurfürstendamm, like Arnold Müller, where my shoes were made. The windowpanes were smashed and 'JUDE' was badly daubed in white on what glass remained.

My father, coming from the East and used to such things, said it was a pogrom and it was time to go. My mother, a Prussian, said we would be all right because her German nationality would guarantee our safety. So we muddled through. Some sent their children to England as happened to Renate Uhry. Her parents, told by friends that a good hiding place for money was in a waterproof bag in the toilet cistern, got so nervous when the Gestapo called that they flushed it down altogether. The Buckys, who owned Karpe, the department store where Grete worked, offered to take me with them to safety in Czechoslovakia. (They left soon after and came to England where I visited them living in style in the fifties in Eaton Square). Frau Bucky's brother went to France and reinvented himself as Marcel Vaudin – his background unknown even to his wife.

And if we were to go, where to go? Some time in 1937 my father took a trip to England, which was not very welcoming to Poles, from Germany with a not very definable profession. So he went to have a look at Seattle, but after his return it was never heard of again. We had by this time put our names down on the quota for immigration visas to the United States. The number of people allowed entry in any particular year was determined by the number of people of their nationality that came to the U.S. in the 1860s. So someone from England would be able to come right away whereas a Hungarian might have to wait 20 years. Your inclusion on the quota would depend either on your passport or your place of birth. So as the German quota was less long than the Polish, my mother and I were put on that in 1936 while my father was on the Polish.

My father had had, for some time, a rumbling appendix. So as we knew it was just a matter of time until we would leave everything behind, he thought it might as well include this troublesome and useless organ. Any money that could be smuggled out would be needed for more dire necessities. My father looked very fine in his hospital bed: dark head on the pillow, hands folded over the sheet and everything else white. There was a picture of a vase of flowers he had painted on the wall. Even though he was there for only a few days, he thought it was too stark to look at a blank wall.

In 1937 a new law was passed that now non-Jews were no longer allowed to work for Jews. As there were no Jewish servants, it meant that overnight no Jewish household had a maid. Amid many tears, the beloved Margarethe, maker of the lightest red currant soufflé omelettes, had to leave. The narrowing of life bore down even on those who could pay to ease their situation.

In the end, the decision was made for us. For one night, on 27th October 1938, there was a tremendous commotion in my parents' bedroom. There was much shouting and banging by Nazi command voices as I had heard on the radio. I lay very low in my bed and wished the rail to prevent my falling out had not been removed years ago. Then all was quiet. Through the window that looked out on to the garden, a little light fell on the familiar pieces in my room. There was the railway line on the floor that my father and I would direct and divert to destinations all over the world. The chair next to my bed in which my mother sat, telling me stories of when she was a little girl in the summer house in Langenau on the

Neisse River and how she, a keen swimmer, would attempt to teach her younger siblings to swim. This took the simple form of throwing first her sister Friedel and then her youngest brother Seppel into the river. Meanwhile her other brother Werner ran along the bank shouting for help. (He had been spared the primitive swimming lesson because when all the children had had diphtheria, he alone was left with a limp). My mother continued by tossing in a few chickens in an attempt to transform them into ducks before help and retribution came. I never tired of hearing that and imagined the house and all the activity that came to an abrupt end during the inflation of 1923 when she was 10 – and it was sold for the proverbial loaf of bread. Another story I liked was about a cooking pot that wore out and got a hole in the base. It had to be thrown away but had another lease of life because the fish in the river into which it was thrown had a happy time swimming in and out. This never failed to move me. I could make out on the floor the pieces of a doll I had taken apart. It had made crying sounds when tipped back and forth and, wishing to discover how that came about, I took it apart. The head was easy and I saw how the long lashed lids opened and shut. The arms were attached to each other through the body by a wire spring affair, as were the legs. And now the small metal box attached to these wires could slip out through the neck cavity and disembodied, it could still make the same sound. I was very enlightened by this discovery. My clothes for the next day lay reassuringly on the day bed at right angles to the wall next to my bed.

So when it was daylight it emerged that my father was gone. Two black-shirted SS men had arrived at 2am. He got dressed – underpants, vest, hand-made shirt, suit, tie, socks, shoes. At the last moment he removed his gold watch and chain and replaced it on the table – as "it was too good for them". He was not alone to have been rounded up. Later that morning my mother went to the Polish Embassy where 17,000 women had converged to be told their alien husbands had been "transported back to their home-land".

The famous Kristallnacht, 9 and 10 November, was different only in degree to all the official vandalism to shops in Berlin. But the time had come for my mother and me to go. So a suitcase each was packed with winter clothes for us to go to Davos. These were ready, along with a return Lufthansa flight ticket each to confound possible suspicion that we were not coming back. A few things were still to be done. It was thought our safety would be greater if we were to be baptised. So it was arranged that a very brave and virtuous vicar of the Anglican church in Berlin anointed us with the holy water to ease our passage into the next world. So we arrived at Tempelhof airport, our two cases, my mother with a bag of all the papers and money and me carrying a last minute whim, a flat Hermes Baby typewriter. There were many border control guards in smart uniforms like khaki riding breeches. Our passports with the Polish eagle on the front – no red 'J' inside – and the round trip tickets. A few years ago a young Israeli friend was cele-brating in Jerusalem. He was jubilant because his Gentile wife, hav-ing recently converted to Judaism, was finally rewarded with a 'J' on her passport: a badge of honour to be displayed with pride. All seemed well until we were in sight of the airplane when I was stopped by an officer. He was charming and told me how pretty I was and what nice clothes I was wearing. I was used to that, so had fortunately not had my head turned when he asked increasingly penetrating questions about the luggage: secret compartments, money in talcum powder boxes, or perhaps in a doll. The plane ride was wonderful and when we saw the zig-zag black and white Alps, it was even more perfect. We arrived at Davos and went to a guest chalet. The owners at first did not want us as they thought our pallor, and coming so early in the season, meant that we were suffering from TB and they were in fear for their children's wellbeing. However, when my mother explained that we were merely tired, we could stay.

CHAPTER TWO
WAITING TO LEAVE

Hedy and Marcelle

So there we were. We went for walks. My mother tried to get the multiplication tables into me. I found 7x very hard when taken out of context. But we had nothing else to do except persevere. In the evening she learned to knit and constructed a pale blue skirt for me – five knit, five purl, so it would not roll up. She even made a little matching jumper and embroidered my initials: 'MW' on it. I loved seeing it upside down when I looked at it when I wore it, still reading 'MW'. We took our meals in the Gasthaus dining room. There were several Germans: some bemoaned the fact they always seemed to miss the celebrations in Germany: first Austria, then Czechoslovakia. This point had eluded me and I puzzled about it to no great effect.

One of the greatest pleasures was the prolonged opportunities for ice skating. Instead of the usual short break in the winter, I grew more proficient as I went almost daily. My skates with a rounded front, with small serrated teeth were buckled on to my brown boots and off I went, with my mother sitting behind the wooden barrier. Either I raced near the edge or did figure eights in the centre of the rink, along with other budding Sonja Henies. We took no notice of the serious old men in their pointy racing skates, arms behind backs, equally in a world of their own. One day I took part in a skating demonstration. Large transparent butterfly wings were attached to my back and I performed in the middle of the empty rink: a backward figure eight on one leg, my whole body bent forward like a T, arms outstretched. The ice had been cleaned before, so I could see the '8' outlined where my skate had etched it.

But now the winter was over and we went to Lausanne and there we were reunited with my father. He had been in an open railway wagon for several days and he and the other men were unloaded at the Polish border. The edited version of his adventure was that the border guard had run out of ink in his official stamp when it was my father's turn with his passport – so the 'No Return to Germany' was only pencilled in on his. So his first – and only purchase in Poland was for an eraser and he duly went back over the border back to Germany as he feared the Germans less than the Poles. Where he went, what he did, how it took nearly a year until he appeared in Lausanne, was never spoken of or even referred to. So there we were. I went to school and my father went to drawing classes, and my mother became less fearful of people knocking on doors. In the evenings my father and I played chess. This had start-ed in Berlin but now we had more time for me to become better at it and to enjoy it more. He did not cheat to let me win but had a handicap of the major pieces: Queen, castle bishops and a knight when we first started. When he began to lose consistently, another piece would be put on for him at the start of the game. It was a tremendous disadvantage for him until he at last started with one castle because without it he could not protect his king. And checkmate was what it was all about: *Schach matt*.

During the day I was at school. I was enrolled at Ecole Vinet at which I was given a large blue and white checked piece of material. This was cut up to make straps that went over the head and longer straps to tie around the waist. These were sewn and turned inside out to hide the stitches and the bottom and top required different stitches to prevent the material from fraying. So it was an apron. In the white boxes at the top, little red Xs were embroidered for decoration in shiny thread and there were more decorations at the bottom above the hem. I had never worn an apron before – though my mother told me she had as a child – but I was pleased to have made it and to take it home.

It was 1939 and our residence permit for Switzerland was running out. So we headed for France which was more tolerant. We were in Menton and everything was colour. There was the blue Mediterranean, the dark green trees, flowers everywhere and sunshine every day. Everything was so beautiful and soft. We flipped stones into the sea. My father was very good at this but I improved with practice. One day I was wandering in a garden that I imagined must have been like Paradise in the Bible when I was stopped by a dark eyebrowed man in a green uniform. Apparently I had strayed into Italy – which without papers I knew to be very grave. I was handed to a French guard in grey and returned to my anxious parents.

Soon after, we moved to Nice. The red carnations from the

market were in a vase on a table every Friday. It was also near the Consulate to check if our number had come up on the quota for a visa to America. The rule was that you could not get a passage on a boat until you had a visa, but you had to use it within six months otherwise you forfeited the position at the top of the ladder and went down to the bottom of the lowest snake. So, weekly, we would join the others of the foreign community in the outer offices of the Consulate.

I attended a ballet class. The mothers sat on stiff chairs around the sides of the room. They watched while a Russian princess and former ballerina took us through our positions. It was totally absorbing and educated one to appreciate a real performance by professionals.

We finally ended in a small house on a hill overlooking the sea in Théoule. There was a huge mimosa bush by the front door and the fluffy flowers amid the spiky leaves gave off a magnificent strong and now evocative scent. On the wooden rail on the balcony I balanced grapes that, after a few days in the sun, turned into sweet warm raisins. I ran over the shingle into the water and my mother taught both my father and me how to swim. Her teaching technique had progressed since Langenau and she held her hand under the diaphragm while we swam until one day the hand was no longer there and we were swimming in the warm, salty blue sea. I was intrigued one day to see a large pink-faced woman selling octopus on the front; she had them on her arm and would pull them off again, leaving red marks from their suction cups on her arm – to show they were wholly fresh.

We lived on the local food. I went out to get a 'flute', the local term for the long French bread, some Brie, and took the empty bottle that was filled from the barrel of the local Algerian wine. Our landlady occasionally called on us, and my father painted a picture for her every month by way of rent. And so the summer went on.

I returned with Tony in the 1950s. I recognised nothing in the new, almost urban environment. The hill in Théoule was littered with villas and Napoule had been upgraded to become La Napoule. The familiar shingle beach was transformed into a sand-box white sand playground. Tony, naturally, thought I had made it all up.

What a summer the one of 1939 was. In my short life in Northern Europe I had never experienced anything like it. It was easy to obliterate the small clouds far out on the horizon. Apart from the idyllic daily routine there were memorable outings. I went to my first opera, Bizet's *Carmen*, performed in the open in Nice. As it got darker in the evening, elephants and horses and goats and dogs came on the vast stage. How wonderful, I thought, to be an opera singer and give so much pleasure to so many people all by oneself, without the help of an instrument. Occasionally my father and I went to Monaco in the mornings, up the hill and into the very grand, deserted gambling palace. I placed my chip on the number of my age of course, which sometimes came up. The casino was huge and awesome, thick carpets, covered tables and the plush curtains drawn against the sun. I could compare it to nothing I had ever seen before; or since, for that matter: gambling palaces are usually full of people and this was the quiet season in a resort in the South of France. I did not know this to be out of the ordinary as I had not experienced the ordinary.

But the summer was coming to an end. One morning I came into the main room of the house to see my mother sitting at the edge of the sofa and in tears. "It is just like 1914" she kept repeating. It was the 1st of September and Germany had just invaded Poland. My father was much more sanguine and not nearly as downcast at the thought of these two enemies destroying each other. It did not, however, end there and soon all of Europe was at war.

The most immediate consequence was that all enemy aliens, in other words many of our German friends, were rounded into detention camps. We visited occasionally, these Spartan, boarding school-like places. We brought chess and other board games as their worst privation seemed to be boredom. My own life was dramatically transformed for the better. I went to school in the neighbouring village of Napoule where I was accorded celebrity status – almost like Joan of Arc – as *la pauvre Polonaise*.

All this overnight, and through no effort or talent on my part making this very puzzling as the reverse might just as easily have happened. School was daily except Thursday and Sunday, days I did not know how to spell in French until many years later. I learned how to take sentences apart with lines underneath, looking rather like long division. In history I learned about the heroine Jeanne d'Arc and her gallant victory over the English. In geography we were given a cardboard outline of France bearing the legend "Enfant voilà ton Pays". We would trace the outline on paper. One week we filled in the rivers, the next the departments, the cities, the mountains, lakes and so on: singly or in various combinations. It remains, to this day, the only country where I can find my way about.

In the playground we played mainly "aux Billes". I started with a bag of small earthen marbles and a larger marble that one flipped with thumb on index finger against the opponent's marble. So it went on until ten earthen marbles qualified for a glass one. These were beautiful with blue or orange whorls inside. One could of course risk all and play with a glass one. Like all games involving balls, it was full of tension and frustrations with cries of 'merde' this and 'merde' that which I soon learned and was ticked off for. As I had no idea what 'merde' meant, I looked it up in the faithful Langenscheidt blue German/French French/German dictionary. There I was unenlightened to learn that 'merde' meant 'Scheiterhaufen'. I looked up 'Scheiterhaufen' and only got back to 'merde'. (Sometimes going back and forth did elicit a word one had heard of). My mother explained a Scheiterhaufen was a compost heap. I was not much wiser.

Although the year was coming to an end, the weather, which I had not distinguished from climate, was glorious. Everyone talked about Noël and "pain d'épices". The special Christmas cake was beautiful, delicious and contained silver charms predicting the coming year's fortunes for the recipient: bell for a wedding, a horse shoe for luck and so forth. It was totally benign, everyone got a charm and all were good fortune. On New Year's Eve my mother and I threw molten lead into cold water to predict the future. This was a traditional German custom where special lead pellets were sold for the purpose. Here we made do with wine bottle tops. The lead was then melted in a spoon over a flame and thrown into a bowl of cold water. The resultant shape, rather like clouds or horoscopes, was susceptible of numerous interpretations: the wish often being father to the vision.

The war in early 1940 was not going well for the Allies, particularly France. From a window of our house that faced the road we saw horse-drawn carts coming from the left piled high, with people sitting on their possessions – mattresses, with pots hanging behind. These carts often came to a standstill as there were many, almost identical horses and carts coming from the Italian border on the right. Even here and even to children it was beginning to look bad.

CHAPTER TWO: MARCELLE

In Nice zig-zag trenches were dug in the park (they had been straight in the First World War) where one was supposed to jump in, in case the Italians (with whom we would not be at war until June 10) dropped their bombs. These trenches were planted with red tulips on either side. We did once see an Italian flying over on one of our regular visits to the Consulate in Nice. He was in an innocent-looking, open cockpit plane, flying so low that his brown leather flying cap was visible. He tossed out a few oval, grey things. We were told they were bombs – grenades more likely by the size. These particular ones in any case failed to explode.

Finally the visas came through and a passage had to be found. Empty though the south of France was of tourists and holidaymakers, it was filled with people wanting to get away. We got a berth on the US Export Line SS Exechorda leaving from Genoa on 1st May 1940. The idea was for my father to come over as soon as his visa on the Polish quota came through, with my mother and me going on ahead so as not to forfeit ours. My mother and I spent one night in a very small room in a small guesthouse in Genoa. A large crucifix hung over the bed and the small brown animals in the bed my mother identified as bed bugs for me. But the next morning we were on the boat to America.

As the ship was not fully booked, we had a lovely cabin with another sitting room next to it. It was just wonderful. Everything was an adventure and if one got lost, there was always a helpful steward to show the way. My mother feared U-Boats and mines but we were after all on an American ship. It was almost America, so we were safe. Even during a very violent storm, when everything creaked and sighed before the bow smashed down, I knew everything would be all right. It was too. We docked at a West Side pier on 10th May 1940 and were in America.

CHAPTER THREE
BECOMING AN AMERICAN

Maurice and Marcelle

We went first to my Uncle Henry who was well established, having been fully resident in New York for two years in an apartment at 360 Central Park West on 96th Street. From there we went to stay with an elderly couple that lived next door at 370. They were very gloomy and said many times that when the war was over they would go back to Germany to be near the grave of their little girl who would have been the same age as me.

While it was being decided what should be done with me, my mother and I explored New York. We went in the subway (like the U Bahn) and in a corner opposite me I saw an old bearded man reading a Yiddish newspaper. This was truly the land of the free – though I still felt at the time I would not have done it so openly.

CHAPTER THREE: MARCELLE

Henry and Erna often had visitors in the afternoon. Erna was a talented pastry cook and her Quetschenkuchen were light and very delicious. This and other pastries and coffee were dispensed in a 'dinette': an extension of the kitchen, which instead of a curtain had a wooden pelmet around the window, painted with fruits and flowers. Hedi Steinberg, an old friend of Erna's who was deserted by her husband very soon after she got married and now worked for the Hebrew refugee organisation HYASS, came often after work. Her son Ronald (later Stanton) and I were shooed into another room to play. We took an immediate dislike to each other. I disliked him because he had blond curly hair like a plate of scrambled eggs, no eyelashes and a southern German accent. He disliked me for being a girl and younger.

Henry came home later from his office in the Continental Ore Corporation at 500 Fifth Avenue, and we would drift away. He once stood himself in front of me and said that he was now, until my father came to America, "*in loco parentis*" and did I know what that meant? It meant, he told me, that he stood in my father's place of authority, which he would test right away by making me cry. I stood more dumbfounded than defiant, unable to understand this rigmarole. Fortunately we were alone so no one else was witness to this bizarre event.

A school was found for me by a friend of my mother's, a Joseph Lieber, who had come to Germany from Galicia where he made a living marketing hair nets made of real hair and was now in New York. He had a friend, a Mr. Leser, who had worked for Unilever in India, but now lived in London, and whose son Michael had been at Cherry Lawn School in Darien, Connecticut for a short while. It had not been possible for me to get one of these scholarships to the Lycée Français in New York as these, reasonably enough, were offered only to French children. Cherry Lawn most generously offered me a place, full tuition and board, completely gratis. Meanwhile my mother found a position as a bookkeeper, for which numbers rather than fluency in English was more of a requirement, for $12 a week. The time passed quite quickly at Cherry Lawn. Everyone was very nice and I skipped from 4th to 5th Grade when the work became increasingly easy.

One holiday I spent with a Dr. and Mrs. Carpinella who lived near the school. They had a little girl aged six or seven for whom I was meant to be a companion – so I was a sort of au pair child. It was a contented family: an uncle appeared one day with a small horse. The uncle wore a huge hat and decorated high-heeled boots. One day we all drove to New York and I sat in the car while the little girl had her blond hair cut at Best's. We all ate together and I slept right at the top of the house with the maids. They were very nice and laughed a lot. It was very cosy up there. There was a basin in the room. I had, however, never seen maids sleep before, nor had I reflected on it.

I returned to New York in the spring of 1941 with great jubilation: my father had arrived – just a year after my mother and me. Much had happened in that time. France had fallen to the Germans on 10th May, soon after we left. The constraints and shortages, even in the south, were also dangerous. When his visa came through, he had to find a passage to New York from Lisbon which required going through Spain, which did not issue visas to the enemies of Germany. So my father and some pals decided to ski through Spain taking rations consisting mainly of sardines and raspberry syrup. My father's efforts were aborted early on when he got pneumonia and had to turn back. But he made it on the second attempt and settled down to wait in Lisbon. This sounded very lively, rather like the descriptions I had heard of Cairo and Casablanca. His ship was rather more crowded than ours had been and many passengers were berthed on the dining-room floor for the night.

But there he was. We were a family once again. We moved into a one-room furnished apartment at 344 West 89 Street. I slept on a bed that folded up and stood behind the door in the kitchen and my parents in the main room. One morning my mother found some black spots on a towel.   She recognised this from her childhood as lice. So after a good shampoo, they were still there but clean at any rate. So we consulted Mrs. Deligtisch. Mr. and Mrs. Deligtisch, their sons Hugo and Manni who we had known in Berlin, had been in America for a few years already. They lived in part of a nice house in Brooklyn. Mr. Deligtisch, who had been a real estate agent in Berlin, now worked in a munitions factory out of patriotism, to stockpile weapons against the Germans, and Mrs. Deligtish made brassieres on her sewing machine for most of the women they knew. By the time she inspected my scalp and pronounced they were indeed lice, they had already migrated to the fresh pastures of my parents.   So we were liberally doused with turpentine and after a few days a very fine-tooth comb removed the eggs. We were free of lice but the turpentine was difficult to budge. several applications of Oxydol washing powder did the trick in these pre-detergent times.

My father took a job as a painter with Leon Decorating Company. He knew he would not be able to practise as an architect until he was a US citizen, so made himself familiar in New York with another aspect of the work he had done in Berlin. One of his early efforts was to paint our apartment. It was full of cockroaches and when they darted about on the ceiling with a white coat of paint they looked far less unappetising.

In the autumn I started school at PS 166, which was very near in walking distance. Every classroom had a deep frieze above the blackboard of the alphabet in capitals and lower case of that beautiful legible round hand that all Americans East/West, North/South have. Would it be too late to emulate? I hoped not.

America's entry into war became more imminent, we counted ourselves the lucky ones. We heard from Grete that she was happy and settled in Buenos Aires. Seppel, my mother's youngest brother, who had worked for my father in Berlin, was now settled as an architect and builder in Sao Paulo, Brazil. After a brief fling with a Brazilian he settled down with Margot and in due course my cousin Marcelo was born. Friedl and her doctor husband, Dr. Cosiner, were in England where eventually my cousins Miriam and Debbie were born. After the war, Friedl and Grete migrated to New York. Seppel remained successful in Saõ Paulo until he died. Werner had been in Palestine since 1938 – now Israel.

My father found a few painters to work for Wegier Decorating Company's office, later Inc, at 151 West 40th Street. It was time to move from the furnished room and at the weekends we went home hunting. We looked uptown as the air was thought to be beneficial to the lungs. There were a very few apartment buildings in Riverdale. There, across the Spuyten Dyvell (spitting devil) at the end of the 7th Ave. Subway line, it was almost like the country – much more so than Grunewald had been. October was the traditional time to move in New York. Many places offered one month's concession of the rent – a depression leftover. Several times we were told that the buildings were 'restricted'. This was then a not common, but not unusual, and not illegal practice of restricting tenants to white Christians. My mother was amazed. She said before Hitler such a practice was unheard of in Germany. But there was plenty of choice and so we looked elsewhere. We eventually found a little, partially furnished house at 42½ Adrian Avenue, over the bridge but still in Manhattan. It was one of a row of small attached houses, part of a very solid Catholic neighbourhood. On our right was a policeman and his family; on our left a taxi driver who washed and polished his taxi most of Sunday with a wonderful substance he called "bonammy" which seemed much more romantic than when I saw it merely as "bon ami" on the tin. Our landlords, Mr. and Mrs. Kent, were going away for a year and we were their first tenants ever. There was a kitchen and dining-room downstairs and a little garden leading from the kitchen, a big living room on the next floor and two bedrooms and bathroom on the top floor. It was very large.

The new school year had started when we moved and I went to PS 7 in the Bronx, a Spartan and disciplinarian establishment. We sat in rows determined by academic results: the best in the front and moving back to the lowest achievers. I hovered between the fourth and fifth row out of six during the two years I attended. In history we were taught about the American Civil War – which seemed a terrible event. But I couldn't make out when it happened or where, but had the highest regard for Abraham Lincoln. He seemed to embody the American Ideal with his humble background and scraggy looks much more than George Washington who marched across the Potomac in a uniform and couldn't tell a lie. Geography was taught by Miss Coyne. She had a long scar on her forearm, allegedly inflicted by a previous student in this rather unruly environment. One of the things she told us was that the houses in Germany were all covered with thatch. We were a mixed lot. The boys mainly delivered groceries in the afternoons and the girls helped out. Eleanor Molino's parents had a soda fountain on Broadway just below the elevated subway line near 242nd Street where we were occasionally treated to a soda at the counter. We were taught domestic science which meant cooking. One week we made a white sauce. I had never eaten, nor even seen, such a substance, and could not fathom the purpose nor discern a taste, but learnt that it had to be smooth. Another course was sewing: tissue paper with holes and darts printed on it was pinned on to material, cut out, basted, sewn together, bias binding around the armholes, button holes made and there at the end of the semester was a flowered blouse. We were to donate our creation to some poor children in Europe about whom we didn't know anything . I thought this an admirable and selfless idea. To this end I went to Woolworths one afternoon and chose a card with clear transparent buttons in the shape of flowers sewn on. I slipped that unnoticed into my satchel, thus in one go marking a rite of passage with a theft from Woolworths, and assuaging my conscience that it was not for my benefit and furthermore thinking it would be for the greatest good and Woolworths would have wished to donate the buttons for such a good cause. Nevertheless my heart was pounding as I left and I decided I was not suited for a career in crime.

The time had come for my teeth to be straightened. They were large and yellow and growing every which way. A very experimental orthodontist was found in Brooklyn who had devised a way to straighten teeth without braces and was looking for volunteers. The first time I went with my mother in a subway to Brooklyn. We changed at Hoyt Avenue and then off at Fordham Avenue where Dr. Jerrold's office was at the corner of Jerome. His system was very simple: the ends of a wire arch were slipped into the little holes on crowns on the back upper molars. There were long hooks on the front; these were attached via rubber bands to hooks on a brown cap that slipped on the head. Needless to say, this was only worn at night. The idea was that the roof of the mouth would thus be broadened and the teeth would slip straight into their proper place, straighten, and therefore could be brushed properly and become white. I went many Saturdays for many years and always liked the change of trains at Hoyt Avenue where there were display windows with clothes and shoes. But in the end it did work and my teeth ended up in a picture in an article in a learned orthodontist journal. For a while I had a little device: a false thin roof of a mouth with a gap and a little key to turn a nut in the middle – to keep the teeth straight.

Sometimes I combined this with visiting the Deligtischs and met up with my parents there. I was growing all the time and I usually came away with a coat the boys had outgrown. Of course it buttoned the wrong way, but no one noticed except me. Then we would drive back in our very unreliable car: a Chrysler convertible, liable to tyre blow-outs and other failures. But it was our first and I loved sitting in the rumble seat with the wind swishing in my hair.

The gift of coats is one example of the refugees helping out by taking in each other's washing. Roman Vishniac, known for his haunting photographs of the vanished life in Poland, came to visit one day and took a photograph of me – looking even more insouciant for not having had my teeth straightened yet. We still have a robust blue and white Meissen group consisting of a healthy girl leading two bulls which we bought from some friends reminiscent to me of an illustration for Goethe's *Hermann und Dorothea*. An acquaintance of ours became a housekeeper – much to everyone's embarrassment, particularly to her employers who did not know how to address her. However, all was well, she married and thus became Mrs. Anneliese Schein and had a son who is now a professor.

Meanwhile I continued at PS 7. For those students who were not up to the academic rigours of the normal curriculum, there was a class sectioned off by age called Junior Industrial, at which the children did not only learn cooking and sewing once a week like the rest of the school, but had lessons daily in woodworking, plumbing and mechanics. But even that must have been quite taxing for some because I once heard a teacher shout at one of the boys that he was so stupid he should go back to where he had come from. I was shocked that this could happen in this haven of the oppressed, in America. I immediately went to the Principal, Dr. Herbert. He was very conciliatory and talked about the heat of the moment and saying things one did not mean and tact. I did not know what he meant, but when I graduated a few years later, I got an American Legion medal for citizenship (although I was not yet a citizen) attached to a purple ribbon, with 1944 on it.

The big event in 1941 was, of course, Japan's attack on Pearl Harbour on Sunday 7th December. The song, "Let's Remember Pearl Harbor as We Did the Alamo" was an instant hit – although I had no idea what or who the Alamo was. But one did know now the war would be won. Flags went up, rationing began for sugar and gas, fences were melted for the war effort, and yellow stars appeared in the windows of the homes of the fallen doughboys. The war created jobs and finally people, even the refugees, became more prosperous.

My father and I went skiing. A bus went very early on a Sunday to Stowe, Vermont and we arrived as it got light, went on the T-bar lifts, skied down on the very hard slopes, and up again. The skiing was much faster than in Switzerland, no powder snow and very,

very cold. But it was very exciting, and we slept all the way back to New York at the end of the day. Once we took a longer break to Mont Tremblant Lodge in Quebec. The skiing was meant to be better there as it was only in its infancy in America. Indeed the Europeans thought they had imported it. The skiing was on trails, dodging slalom-like between trees, even colder and faster than Vermont. It was very exhilarating. In the evening we sat in a huge dining hall, quiet as a cathedral, with wooden beams and gold decorations on the ceiling. My father gazed at the other silent diners and said, "You know, I think we are the only ones." How were we or the hotel to have known? It is not as though we were called Finkelstein from New York; but we never returned.

Our life continued to be very private. My parents worked all week and came home to find me either doing my homework or winding a huge mahogany victrola. I was not encouraged to make friends at school, though there was one German boy, Arnold, in my class who thought he would be helping the war effort by refusing to speak German with his parents. I did not understand the connection. To play ball, or roller skate or hop-scotch with the children in the street was, of course, out of the question. But in keeping with a government edict, I cultivated a Victory garden. Carrots and radish seeds were sown in rows delineated by the picture on the Burpees packets of seed and soon grew and stood like soldiers. On a slope at the back I grew nasturtiums that tumbled down in their Provençal colours. On Sunday morning we ate *matzobrei* and my father explained how it should be made having enjoyed it as a child. It was indeed difficult for it not to be delicious: egg-soaked matzoh poured on to sizzling butter in a pan and flipped over to brown the other side.

My life at PS 7 was confined to school and did not spill over to after-school. I had a blue lunch box and a thermos like the other people and its contents we consumed in the auditorium. Everyone had a nickname, so I decided to have one too: it was TERRY and to emphasise this I had it stencilled on the head of a horse that I pinned on to my chest. Somehow it lacked conviction and so no one was persuaded that Terry was really meant to be me.

My education continued at PS 7. The term after making a blouse we made a skirt, then a dress. The consummation of our dressmaking skills was the graduation dress we made when we had completed 8B and would go to High School. The material for this was traditionally white organdie, but there were war shortages and it was thought to be more patriotic to save white for brides. I chose mauve organdie to be decorated with crucially placed deeper mauve velvet bows. Naturally we had had the same pattern for style, and with the sweetheart neckline and puffed sleeves, I think we all looked stunning.

1944 marked not only my graduation from PS7 but also my last year at summer camp. This was (before Dr. Jonas Salk made it redundant by his vaccine) in Maine where not only was there no polio but no snakes or poison ivy. The one my mother found for me was called Les Chalets Français where I not only had a scholarship but also kept my French fresh. We went up in a sleeping car to Bangor, Maine, and arrived in the morning and were driven to Deer Isle. We lived in log cabins like Abraham Lincoln, rode horses, did archery, swimming, and made leather belts. It was very nice indeed. The meals were determined by the days of the week: Boston beans on Saturday, camp fire on Sunday with marshmallows and ice cream which had been churned in a machine surrounded with salt for the cream to freeze. On Sunday blue felt on green banners were awarded for Français, Natation or Esprit de Corps.

We also made balsam fir cushions for our parents and hoped we would return the following year.

From then on my education became less passive. I had hoped after PS7 to go to Hunter High School, a very competitive and academically highly graded city school in midtown Manhattan. I was, however, not accepted, which as things turned out was the best that could have happened, for my mother was told that the most academic school in New York was Fieldston.

When she telephoned the school to arrange for me to be admitted there, she told the person at the other end that we had not been in America for very long. The person then snootily asked whether I could speak English and my mother replied "Yes; and French and German, too."

CHAPTER FOUR:
HIGH SCHOOL

Marcelle and friend, winter 1935

Fieldston was part of the Ethical Culture complex which provided education from pre-kindergarten through high school. It was founded at the beginning of the 20th Century for children whose parents did not wish them to have a parochial education or were unable to attend more traditional schools because of a fairly exclusive *numerus clausus*. This meant that the majority of children were Jewish but there were also many means-tested scholarships. The Ethical Culture did not impinge on the academic side at all but we all had an ethics class weekly where large ethical problems were debated. Our class was often led by Algernon D. Black and we discussed warfare, mercy killings, animal experimentation and other unresolvable problems with both right and wrong on each side.

The academic side opened a new world. I was, like Caliban, amazed at how much there was, also that knowledge was not finite. I learnt Latin with all the neat constructions and compressed sentences. I decided to expand and took Greek (mainly because the very handsome David Franklin was also going to be a part of this small class). I learnt about biology and dissected multi-coloured dogfish and then moved on to rats. These looked very drowned in their individual jars of formaldehyde. Mine was a female and very little of it was left at the end of the semester. I liked it but had little talent for biology and one's hands peeled off terribly from the formaldehyde. The really talented ones like Petra McElwee and Linda Shapiro were encouraged to do 'creative writing' and invented stories that they wrote down adding, to my amazement, to the existing body of literature. But my greatest love was chemistry. It had everything: the physical equipment and the possibility of transforming the universe. We made electricity, water and compounds like hydrogen sulphide with hydrogen and sulphur, each of us with a test tube and Bunsen burner. It was both logical and surprising. We grew crystals, the easiest first like copper sulphate, and common salt later. A most wonderful teacher, Martha Munzer – a former Fieldston pupil – shared our enthusiasm as though she too were discovering the world of chemistry for the first time. It was in the physics laboratory next door that J. Robert Oppenheimer solved his first equations in physics.

On the non-academic side we did various kinds of art. We threw clay on a wheel which one turned with a foot pedal rather like a sewing machine, and brightly glazed ashtrays and vases soon adorned our home. It was really too easy and I considered it child's play, also better done by machines.

Much more to my taste was the construction of portrait

heads in clay. Bernard Werthman showed me how to roll the clay into snakes. Laying them on top of each other: first you had a neck, then extending forward you built up the chin and back of the head, then up until you got to the mouth, more forward the nose, the eyes, then move back for the forehead. The whole head was hollow and the ideal was to have it no more than half an inch thick to prevent cracks when firing. Between sessions the clay was kept damp with moist rags – in those pre-plastic days. One aimed for an Aristotelian mean: too damp and the head collapsed into cow pat shape, not damp enough and new additions of clay for ears or eyebrows would not adhere. I found it both challenging and yet easy. So I undertook to make the allied triumvirate. I started with a head of Stalin, which I made in terracotta, then a head of Churchill in grey clay, and ended with a head of Roosevelt in white. These I felt were my contribution to world peace and understanding, which I fervently hoped would follow. To further knowledge of the workings of the body, I went to the Art Student's League on 57th Street on Saturdays. There very patient nude models stood or sat stock still for hours with very few breaks – while charcoal drawings were made by the students. The teachers were uniformly encouraging and would point at the drawings, but never touched or improved them. I had little talent in this medium and no amount of smudging produced anything anyone would wish to look at twice. Getting the proportions right is not sufficient to create art. Meanwhile on Saturday morning my father was painting beautiful compositions of south of France flowers in vases or bowls of fruit. This he did under the supervision of Suzanne Schülein who painted under her maiden name of Suzanne Carvalho. The Schüleins had left Germany very late and now lived extremely modestly on her earnings from what was once a hobby, having previously lived very comfortably from the proceeds of her husband's brewery business. When my father was not staying for lunch with the Schüleins we would go to the Russian Tea Room where I always had an open red caviar sandwich on the blackest pumpernickel bread.

The sport was divided by season: swimming and basketball in the winter and hockey in the fall. My European breast stroke was not competitive with the American crawl and I could not unlearn these froglike movements hard as Pat Katzenstein, the phys-ed coach, tried. I liked playing right wing in hockey, way out on my own and yet part of a team, but never approached the prowess of the stars Nai-Shun Chang, Patra McElwee and Helen Hays. We were very much encouraged to do something musical and one term I joined the choir where, under the direction of Bernard Werthman, about fifty of us learnt to sing Fauré's Requiem. I was a very non-demanding alto. We met weekly to go through the whole work and then phrase-by-phrase until we understood every note and every word. It had not occurred to me how much thought went into not only the composition but also the performance. To this day I cannot hear a production of this moving work without wishing to join in. Fieldston was a tolerant school, encouraging one to undertake things even if one was not good at them.

The social side was less straightforward. Most of the pupils lived on the Upper West Side and came up on the subway, getting out at the last stop at 242nd Street and then walking up the hill to the Riverdale campus. We were still living in Adrian Avenue, so although I had a very short trip to school, I saw my fellow students only at school and not at the daily commute nor at the weekends. We all had lunch together in the gymnasium hall. Who was to sit at which table was predetermined to break up cliques and prevent anyone from being left out. The food was not too unusual and pretty recognisable, chicken, rice, fruit salad, ice cream. But the pattern of life was soon to change, again for the better.

It was 1944 and apartments were now not so easy to find. The Kents wanted to return to their little house and my parents wanted to move back into midtown to be nearer work. Advertisements in the New York Times and agents brought nothing for a year until we found a beautiful apartment at 200 West 58 Street. This, although on the corner of 7th Avenue, overlooked the park because directly below on Central Park South was a riding school over whose low roofs we saw the green trees in the summer and the bare branches in the winter. There was an entrance hall and a large living room leading with double doors to a dining room with a vast kitchen and a small maid's room behind. A bedroom for my parents from a little back hall, my room and a bathroom with a window between. There were huge high ceilings and lovely mouldings. And all high up in the sky on the 10th floor. There were dignified elevator men in uniform for the front and the service elevator – also a doorman under an ornate canopy. There was very little to leave behind in Adrian Avenue except the lines on the wall to mark my growth, which the Kents liked to keep, as they had no children. The bone structure was pretty luxurious but of course we had no furniture. So we went to auction houses and carpet shops to look for the sort of furniture that we had been used to and very soon it looked as though we had always lived there. I chose to have my room painted pink with a bit of mauve in the panels. My father said I would not like it for long; he was right but indulged me all the same. I had a beautiful bed with an arched headboard surrounding caning, and a white painted kneehole desk that I have to this day.

On Saturdays my mother and I would often go shopping for clothes. My first purchase, soon after I went to Fieldston, was a beige teddy bear coat with brown piping and wooden buttons which buttoned the right way. It was my first new piece of clothing since leaving Germany four years before. This had a matching cap that tied under the chin. This was the height of fashion, chic and an elegant, discreet and ungaudy colour. Our shopping sometimes took us to Loehmanns in Brooklyn. This was run by the very ancient Mrs. Loehmann, who had helped designers during the depression and they now thanked her by giving her first refusals on over-produced or end of season's discounted lines. The front room had dresses and suits marked down to $10 or less from a heady $50. But it was the Back Room, furnished in Moorish taste with armchairs and antique chests, that was the goal. Everybody's ideal was to find a Trina Norell for $30 in the Back Room. There were no changing rooms. One tried on among the racks, with Mrs. Loehmann – very old and wrinkled – watching along with other dragons to make sure the dresses were pulled over the head and not stepped into, and to discourage shoplifting. It was totally wonderful and absorbing, and induced a reverse cost ambition and a boastfulness about how very little one had paid: a full turquoise silk skirt with silver embroidery, with matching high-heeled pointed mules, teamed with a V-necked jumper of matching hue, all for $35 – never mind when it would be worn. I hadn't felt so elegant since I had a blue velvet dress as Esther, for Purim, when I was 5.

I often went to the Metropolitan Museum where I immersed myself in the Egyptian rooms and squeezed into the little tombs and gazed at the calm, beautiful faces of a lost civilization from which these relics had been saved. They looked so calm, benign, regal and domestic – had one of them been Haman? One seldom got an answer to the questions that were really puzzling. I loved the Planetarium. There in a darkened room one saw the dome of stars for the particular evening of the day one was there. The Big Dipper, Cassiopeia, the Seven Sisters, Taurus, and, when the whole night sky for that day was shown and dawn replaced the stars and moon, the invisible narrator wished us good morning. Imagine gazing at the brilliance of a star whose light was reaching us from millions and millions of years ago.

I still helped in the office on Friday afternoons although we had moved to larger premises way on top of the Commodore Hotel on 42nd and Park above Grand Central Station. I checked the money in the envelopes for the painters' wages that my father would then deliver, with his youngest salesman Bob. (When it was discovered later that my father was too old and Bob too young to qualify for insurance in case of hijack, this antiquated practice was abandoned in favour of cheques). On weekends I would often go with my father to see the jobs that were done in non-office hours like banks, shops (Bonwit Teller, Ovington's, Henri Bendel) and a really huge job of redecorating the whole of the Paramount Theatre, which required vast high scaffolding. My father did the gigantic ceiling in a salmon pink colour, much to the despair of Mr. Pleschette, the manager. But my father said he would do it only in that colour or not at all and reassured Gene Pleschette that if he was not absolutely delighted, the whole thing would be repainted for free. Fortunately all was well or we would surely have gone bankrupt. I gained some credibility with my friends by getting lots of tickets for shows at the Paramount. I felt I earned my keep a bit while the job was in progress because one day, walking past on my own I saw some signs for a rival firm (who were in fact quite legit- imately painting up some of the lavatories or something) all of which I meticulously removed. We went to the Polo Grounds, home of the New York Giants, which we painted, very calm and quiet as I never saw it filled with fans. My father was asked to paint the Florida Pavilion for the World's Fair, which was having a new lease of life. Believing this to be a negatively profitable proposition, yet unwilling to deliver a refusal, he made an estimate so high that even if full payment was not forthcoming, all would still be well. Needless to say he did not get the job and Florida defaulted on all the refurbishments to its pavilion. The painters were a highly skilled union, using the finest pigs' bristles from China and were wonderful to watch. The head foreman was Mr. Weintraub who, when not working, wore a cashmere coat and a handmade hat and drove a Buick – a new model each year. Even smaller and even more exclusive and skilled was the paperhangers' union. The best paperhanger in New York worked for my father, a Mr. Buchwald. He was sorry his son Art did not follow him into a safe job but chose the less secure road of journalism. One of the most pleasing jobs was the New York Times, which got us the Book Review and Magazine on Thursday – almost like getting the result before the race.

I now joined the others on the subway to Fieldston, although I got on the Local at 59th. There was always a familiar face when I changed to an express at 72nd Street. Then along under Central Park West 86th, 96th under Harlem 103rd but above ground at 125th, down again 136th, and up again for the last few stops until 242nd, end of the line. The trains were never full in either direction as we were going against the commuter flow. At school we still divided pretty much girls and boys although there were some fast ones like Freda Gould who paired off with Paul Nessiter and Helen Hays, who loved and eventually even married James Ginsberg (later Gordon) and Ellen Rosenthal who dated college boys from very early days. It was she who dispensed rides back to

Manhattan after school. Her father owned Riverside Memorial –
the leading funeral service in New York – and would send a car to
pick up Ellen from school. This was quite often a mourner's car or,
better still, the actual hearse car – with benches all around the sides
and of course the space in the middle for the coffin quite empty.
There we would be, giggling away while the passengers in the
neighbouring cars on the highway lowered their eyes or even
doffed their hats. Helen Hayes and Ellen were, with Joan Chanin,
the most beautiful and popular girls in the class and were effortless-
ly good at everything, and also very nice. Others, not so pretty had
their 'noses done' mainly in their sophomore year when at 16 they
had stopped growing. So they retained their large dark eyes and
seductive lips, but the noses were now less fearsome, a transformation for the better – the face, the character, everything was
improved – and they probably achieved better results on their SATs
too.

The class had now been together for three years and we moved
as a swarm. Naturally in the background loomed college, but
meanwhile we had grown up confident that we could face the
world and possibly even improve it. Helen Hays invited the whole
class to her parent's house at Annandale on Hudson. It was high up
and the river could be seen below. We suddenly became children
again, picnicking on the grass, playing ball games, swimming and as
wer were helping it was our picnic. We were told not to stack the
plates by Helen's mother so as not to get the back of the plate dirty
in these pre-dishwasher days.

When we became seniors it was traditional for the class to
make a visit to Washington. This would bring us closer to 'our' her-
itage. By this time it was mine too, for in May 1946, in the District
Court at Columbus Circle, I was sworn in as a U.S. citizen. My first

privilege was that I could change my name, which I immediately took advantage of and changed it from Marcella to Marcelle. I thought this was much more sophisticated and it has been my name ever since. As I was attending school it was assumed I was literate and knew some American history. Not so for my parents. When it was my father's turn, one of the questions he was asked was "who was the first president of the United States?" When he answered "Lincoln" he was still awarded the prize. Perhaps he perceived a deeper truth that the tall craggy intelligent homespun from Springfield, Illinois was more the father of the Union than the English landowning general in an embroidered uniform. To go to Washington: we would travel by train and stay in various hotels and look at the Lincoln Memorial, the White House and Congress. But Walter Winter, the only coloured pupil in our class, would, under the laws that still held in the south even in the nation's capital, of course be staying with friends. He took this in his stride, as it seemed perfectly natural to him and he was looking forward to seeing the sights during the day – the Jeffersonian inscription: "All men are created equal" and spending the nights with his friends. I am afraid that I funked it and didn't go. Having come to America new and learnt it from the outside, without instincts or background, I could not reconcile the conflict of principle and practice.

Our life kept pace with the country's prosperity. We acquired a cook, a Swiss lady who used to work for Henry and Erna, but resented the uniforms she had to wear there. She made wonderful mushrooms in cream sauce for us, which we all loved and had nearly every day. She never stopped talking and indeed was the cause of my father's swift recovery from a broken foot. For as he lay in bed, a captive audience with a cast going up to his hip, Olga stood in the doorway. So he got up and out into his car and could drive as it was his left foot that was broken and with automatic gears he needed only his right to drive.

My parents went to the Metropolitan Opera at 40th Street on alternate Mondays. My mother, who was very musical, loved it and the dressing up. My father would ask "how many dead" at the start of the performance and count. The opening of the season was very gala and many men still appeared in white tie.

It had only been a matter of time, but finally the war in Europe did come to an end and the longed-for peace began. It was now possible for Grete to come to New York from Buenos Aires. While there she had acquired a rather pathetic husband – but he was at least a husband. After various attempts at other activities he was finally ensconced in a shop selling lampshades and we had a surfeit of them from his premises on Lexington Avenue. Grete was a first class competent bookkeeper and was immediately installed in Henry's office. Friedl and her husband Dr. Cosiner came from England where Miriam and Debbie had been born. He had to retake his medical exam but Friedl could start work right away as a nurse. Seppel, handsome and charming with a light touch of almost a playboy, came from Saõ Paulo bearing a gold aquamarine ring for me. (This, on her 21st birthday, I passed on to his son Marcelo's daughter Carol). All the fun took its toll and he died too soon, leaving a widow and Marcelo under ten years old. (Marcelo eventually became my legal ward, went to school in England, then moved to Switzerland. There he married the lovely Judith who had been born in Auschwitz, had two children, a dog and a barbecue). Another very distant connection, Erich (now Eric) Lomnitz, came from Chile to settle in New York to work for Henry. The Leirs had now moved to a larger apartment in the Majestic – a Chanin build-

ing – 115 Central Park West at 72nd Street. A real interior design-
er decorated it, and much of the furnishings were made in France,
including a large armoire that had been dismantled to become a
doorway between the dropped living room (approached by two
stairs from the hall) and the study. They had acquired a large house
made of grey stones with lots of acres in Ridgefield, Connecticut,
where they went on weekends. There my uncle constructed roads
and lakes. The two acres offered to us were never taken up. My
father was more tempted by the sea and in any case, my uncle, a
short bald German with glasses, was not at ease with my tall handsome father with dark wavy hair. This tension between Eastern
Jews – from Russia or Poland – and those from Germany began to
ease after the war. A well-known Jewish club, the Harmonie, which
had been exclusively for Jews of German descent, was touting for
members after the war. When my father was approached, he
declined on the grounds that he did not join clubs. Nevertheless
my parents' social situation had changed. My mother, after all, had
been the fine German Jew when they were in Germany. But now
my father was the dominant figure.

When the office of Wegier Decorating Co. Inc. had moved to
the Commodore it became a tradition to give a party there at
Thanksgiving. This was mainly for customers but also a number of
private 'Leute' (as my mother once called them in a letter to me).
There were drinks of course, and smoked salmon, an orchestra and
several hundred guests. After the party Sid Gordon would take the
favoured suppliers to the Brass Rail Restaurant to continue the
merrymaking. Sid had become my father's top assistant. He had
been an upholsterer when he met my cousin Marysza. She and my
father's brother Kiwe and his wife survived Auschwitz and came to
New York as soon as the war was over. Kiwe looked a bit like my

father but seemed much, much older. Marysza too had the same fine nose.When she and Sid were on honeymoon in Florida, someone on the beach asked what the numbers on her forearm were – she said it was her telephone number. She had retained the Auschwitz tattoo for a while because it meant she had not collaborated with the guards, but eventually it was removed. Sid was a great fixer. He always had a stash of ballpoint pens when they first came out and were very rare.Years later he found a watch for our son Edward that on the reverse had all the workings shown behind a transparent panel.

The other main feature of our senior year was the endless discussion, speculation about college applications.There were many imponderables on which this depended. Not only the work we had been doing for four years, but also the SAT college entrance exams, the extra curricular activities, the recommendations from the teacher – and what clout they had with the colleges, the number of people applying to a particular college and the reputation Fieldston had with a college on the basis of previous students – and of course, just plain luck.

So in the spring of 1948 the envelopes started to arrive. Rather like making custard: good if is thick, bad if it is thin.We were told that this was a particularly difficult year because of the GI Bill of Rights allowing free college education to returning veterans. So this made the disappointed feel better as it did those who were admitted to the college of their choice. I had the good luck to be admitted to Bryn Mawr, which, being a Quaker foundation, had on principle no *numerus clausus* and admitted students on merit alone. When later, under the McCarthy persecutions, many colleges refused to employ or even dismissed staff for ideological reasons, Bryn Mawr stood firm. I was lucky to have been taught Greek literature by Richmond Lattimore (brother of the communist Owen) whom no other college would look at. It was the Quakers who during and after World War I sent food packages to Germany. My mother and family were one of the many beneficiaries of this forgiving generosity to enemies. She told me when the packages arrived each child would be given a carrot to dip into a jar of jam to eat. Henry, she said, would only lick the jam off while the others obediently bit the carrot thus reducing the amount of jam!

CHAPTER FIVE
COLLEGE

Marcelle circa *1941*

Bryn Mawr extended the horizon that Fieldston had first revealed. There were girls from all over the country, some like Rosemary Haines from the south who had never seen snow. Many had never seen a European: we were only three in those pre-global days - Francine du Plessix – now Gray; Katusha Cheremeteff – now Davison, and me. But the view of culture and learning was global and we studied and learnt a lot and loved it. We were taught by the professors and not graduate students finishing their theses – Dr Chew for English; Dr. Berliner for Chemistry, Professor Brée for French, Milton C. Nahm for Philosophy, Caroline Robbins, sister-in-law of Lord Robbins of the Robbins Report for History. (When her deaf, eccentric husband Dr. Herben, who taught us Middle English and *The Canterbury Tales*, met my fiancé Tony, he turned on his hearing aid upon learning he was a Fellow of All Souls and said, "Judas Priest, those babies are tough, you have to be bright to get in there").

Bryn Mawr was pretty isolated. The nearest college was Haverford, another Quaker foundation, with whose serious men we sometimes shared classes in recondite subjects. Further along – not on the main railway line – was Swarthmore, a co-educational college known as the little Quaker Matchbox, whose brainy pupils kept very much to themselves. (This was confirmed later when Tony taught there for a semester and said they were the cleverest and hardest working undergraduates he had ever encountered.) So like families in remotest Yorkshire in the 19th Century we fell back on our own inventions. Joanna Semel, my best friend (now Rose) ran a literary magazine called (we thought very cleverly) Counterpoint and she was brilliantly imaginative, not only soliciting original works from undergraduates and even professors, but also in getting a vast subscription list. All of this fell down as fast as it had risen when she passed the reins on to me. To make some extra money I tutored people to get them through the required oral exams in two foreign languages. My sales pitch was money back in case of failure, but double the going rate. I made sure of success with plenty of tutorials. My other enterprise was Rock Laundry: a system of collection of dirty and delivery of clean laundry from the Halls of Residence. I managed to get a weekly public announcement made at lunch in the halls so had a monopoly of a somewhat imperfect service. As a member of the swimming team, I was in a good position to help Joanna to qualify for her degree by passing a swimming test. I subjected her to the same sure method my mother had used on me and my father years before. She succeeded and graduated in English Literature *summa cum laude* (the first for many years in this difficult subject) and I was proud of the surrogate part I played in her success. For more serious pleasures we went along the Paoli local to Thirtieth Street in Philadelphia and from there took the train to New York. People said of Philadelphia in those days that they had been there but it was closed. This was never put to the test except for a lugubrious dinner with a boy to mark the end of a romance which had hardly begun.

In the summer of my third year, Joanna persuaded our parents to let us go to England to do a course in Shakespeare, in his birthplace of Stratford. I loved summer school. I had enrolled the year before for a course at the Sorbonne with Elaine Marks, which was run by Miss Brée. During my first summer I had gone to Harvard where we stayed in Eliot House and had ice cream every evening, funded by an 'ice cream bequest' by a benign former Harvard student.

Very soon after our arrival, Joanna and I rerouted the taxi after we took one unimpressed look at Swiss Cottage where Mr. and Mrs. Leser had proposed to find somewhere to put us up. So we ended up in a small, clean, discreet, well-appointed house in Seymour Street, not far from Marble Arch. We had delicious breakfasts of egg and toast (still rationed for the general populace) and the other guests, all ladies, kept very late hours. We naturally believed, romantically, that we were staying in a high-class house of low repute. One day, after buying armfuls of flowers at the crack of dawn at Covent Garden on the day before setting off for Stratford, I had to go to a wedding. This came about because my mother's secretary, Ruth Guggenheimer, had a sister Hellen who was marrying an Englishman, Sir Keith Joseph. Having missed the ceremony through flower buying, I did get to the reception where one of the 600 guests offered me a glass of champagne – at 3.30 in the afternoon! I had never heard of such a thing and opted for iced coffee. This man Tony Quinton I thought he said was his name – then whisked me off to another wedding, of Marcus and Cecilia Dick. He then dropped me off at Marble Arch (I thought my address might be a well-known brothel and I did not wish to give the wrong idea). He said he had to pick up his mother who was sitting in Hyde Park surrounded by her luggage having arrived from Canada that morning. He said he had to go to Scotland for a long weekend. Nothing had been written down so it all went out of my head until indeed I was invited to Oxford – which I thought was very beautiful although I thought all the buildings were churches. We went to a production of *Samson Agonistes* in a quad in All Souls at which I nearly died of cold – it being August. So although I had been meant to stay two nights I thought I had better go back to Stratford. Finding my hotel paid for at the Randolph, I was so mortified I invited this Tony to Stratford for the following weekend. We went on the river there too, and somehow that was it. So at the end of the summer I went back to Bryn Mawr to finish my final year and told my parents my intention to get married. This was not greeted with enthusiasm. Much pressure was brought to bear on me to dissuade me. My father went no further than to say that he knew all about English people: he used to see couples sitting after dinner in the lounges of the hotels in Europe. They sat, man and wife, after dinner not speaking a word, just reading. Then the husband would nod and they both went upstairs. My mother was altogether more energetic and sent me to a psychologist who asked me if I really wished to get married, so I said yes and that was an end of it. In 1952 Isaiah Berlin was delivering the Flexner Lectures at Bryn Mawr. He brought letters from Tony and

I helped him pack his trunk. On the mantelshelf in his room at the Deanery, which I needed special permission to visit, he had about half a dozen jars full of kumquats in syrup. I eventually found out that he took them out only as far as his fingers could descend into the jar, his great mind not thinking either of decanting or even using a spoon. My mother appealed to him to intervene and he spoke later of her dark brown eyes gazing into his. As a friend of Tony's he declined to interfere.

Tony came for a short visit during this final year. He met my father in a neutral environment. The encounter was amicable but unyielding and firm on each side. During his visit to Bryn Mawr we were invited for dinner with his god-mother in Chestnut Hill. Eugenia Fuller Atwood's parents and Tony's mother's parents (Dr. and Mrs. Jones) were friends, living in Victoria. Their other child, Richard (Dick) Fuller had a romance with Aunt Ruth but she was firmer with small decisions and could not make the big one. He consoled himself by founding a museum of Chinese art in Seattle. Uncle Jack and Aunt Eugenia were profoundly public-spirited people, living in Chestnut Hill where he ran the hospital's trustee board and Aunt Eugenia built the church. So we went to this enormous white house and were really welcomed. Two little dogs ran around loose and after settling in, we assembled in a room with carpets and lamps and little tables. I was handed a large glass with ice and what I thought was water that I duly drank – being ice cold it had little flavour. It was not until we were halfway through dinner that I realised it must have been gin or something like that and that I was completely and totally drunk. They were used to strong waters, even during prohibition they had their bootleg liquor delivered by the policeman. I was still sensible enough to know that if I stayed absolutely silent I would not say anything wrong and disgrace myself forever. So after dinner we removed to an analogous room to the pre-dinner one, me still silent until it was time to go upstairs to the room of their daughter Leila, who was also at Bryn Mawr. There in the beautiful bathroom with a dolphin to fill the bathtub, I was very, very sick, but did not make any mess. The next morning I was quite sprightly, the dogs were exercising in a cage outside, the Irish maids in their lace aprons and little lace fillets on their hair served the cereal out of jars into which it had been decanted, and Uncle Jack and Aunt Eugenie asked how we had slept. It was a beautiful, calm, responsible world I had not even imagined. They took me on unquestioning and immediately as an honorary relation which we remained until they died.

So in June 1952 after graduation I eloped and was met in Southampton by Tony (who after all this time I feared I might not recognise). I had had a bit of trouble getting landed by the immigration official on the boat. He asked for 'proof' that I was indeed getting married, explaining that many girls came in saying just that – early asylum seekers. The letters from Tony, which he read out deadpan: the dinner menus at All Souls, A.L. Rowse being tiresome, were unconvincing. So he compromised and landed me for six weeks and I riposted with bravado, "If I don't marry him I'll marry someone else." But it all ended happily, Tony's mother was very welcoming considering her darling only son's intended in-laws found him wanting, and we lived happily ever after.

In 1954 we took a trip to New York and all was forgotten. Joanna was born in 1955 and Edward Frith in 1957. Joanna's children, Sarah Elizabeth in 1982, Thomas Nathaniel 1984, Jane Meredith 1987, Grace Ellen 1988 and Mary Catherine 1990; and Edward's children Olivia Rose 1991, Ella Suzannah 1994, Rupert Frith 2005 and Benedict Nicholas Maurice in 2007.

TONY

CHAPTER ONE
A NAVAL CHILD

Tony in Malta circa *1929*

I was born on 25th March 1925 in a fairly ugly terraced house called Thelmadene in Gillingham, Kent. We were living there because my father, a naval doctor, was stationed at Chatham, one of the country's three great naval ports, along with Portsmouth and Plymouth. Naturally, I remember nothing of my life in Gillingham since we left it after a short time when my father was posted to Malta. My mother used to speak very warmly of the 'monthly nurse' who helped to look after me. But such benefit as I received from her did not extend to any conscious recollection. My father, Richard Frith Quinton, had been born in 1889 in London where his father, also Richard Frith, was first a prison doctor and later a moderately reforming prison governor. My father went to school at Berkhamsted and then on to do his medical training at the London Hospital in Whitechapel where his father had been before. He qualified just before the outbreak of war in 1914 and soon joined up as a naval doctor. He served, I think, principally in the Mediterranean and was sunk there in the HMS Majestic in 1916, setting an example for me to follow later.

My grandfather, whom I knew and greatly loved in his advanced old age, was a good natured and humorous man with the moustache of his epoch and a bald head. When I was going to bed while staying with my grandparents, I used to take my leave of him by kissing him at the topmost point of his bald head, sometimes causing him to jump when I approached him unseen since he was by this time totally deaf. He had been born in Enniskillen, Northern Ireland, one of the many sons of a wine merchant there. The eldest son, James Wallace, rose rapidly in the Indian civil service until he was murdered in Assam by a deranged Rajah. The death was avenged by a punitive expedition, the offending Rajah was hanged and a statue of my great-uncle was erected in the middle of the region's capital, Manipur. I was told by an Englishman who had stayed on in India after Independence in 1947 that it was still standing in the 1950s. My grandfather's brothers took progressively lower status jobs but one of them, Maurice, was a fairly distinguished county cricketer, earning his living as a schoolmaster.

My grandfather was a great admirer of the writings of Stephen Leacock, his collection of whose works I still have. His humour was of a pleasantly Leacockian kind. For one birthday he gave me, amongst other things, a Woolworth's notepad costing one penny, inscribed with advice. I remember one item: "always put off 'til tomorrow what you do not absolutely have to do today". I have profited from this for many years. He died in 1934 aged over 80.

His wife, my grandmother, born Rose Symonds, was a tiny

little woman of great determination, possibly in some eyes a bit of a tyrant. But to me she was endlessly kind: putting me up, for example, when my mother was away, when we would play bezique together on a green baize tablecloth in the evenings. She let me listen to whatever I liked on the Pye wireless set in what was known as 'the study' and I steadily tuned in to Children's Hour at 5.15 every evening. She had been born in Quetta where her father was an army chaplain at the time. In retirement at Twyford, near Winchester, she was deeply involved with various good works. She was an ardent supporter of a Miss Pesel who founded something called the Yew Tree Guild, which produced beautiful tapestry covered kneelers for Winchester Cathedral. The Women's Institute frequently gathered in our garden and from my room upstairs I would join in the singing of 'Jerusalem' with which the meetings began.

She had three sons and a daughter, all of whom were in some ways involved with the Indian sub-continent. Uncle Bill was a civil engineer who made a very good second marriage after the death of his first wife, and lived in Compton, a village quite near Twyford. Uncle Hal passed from Brasenose College (where he was known as 'Quinners') into the Indian civil service, which he had to leave early because of deafness. Once the governor lent Hal his ivory-covered train. Some discontented Indian threw a bomb at it and my uncle said, "Please make less noise in the kitchen," acquiring a reputation for bravery. He too ultimately settled in the outskirts of Winchester at St. Cross. Aunt Dorothy, a highly intelligent woman, married a very nice but rather foolish man who was a tea planter in Ceylon. It was just as well that he had substantial private means since I do not imagine he could have been any good at it.

They left Ceylon after a few years because my aunt could not stand the heat. Uncle Jack, her husband, was a very good companion for young children. Once in Cornwall when we were on holiday there with his family, he took us all for a ride round the harbour at Looe in a wonderfully smart motorboat, an outing which cost half a crown. We then did it twice again, a prodigality I greatly admired.

In the post-war years my father served for some time on the HMS Hood, the pride of the navy and at 42,000 tons, its largest ship. During the course of this posting my father went on a world cruise on the Hood calling at British naval ports all over the globe. Among them was Esquimault near Victoria, British Columbia on the west coast of Canada. He took with him a letter of introduction to a Dr. O.M. Jones who had married a sister of the wife of an admiral of whom he was some sort of protégé, perhaps because of the quality of his jokes. Among Dr. Jones's five children there was one over-elaborately named Gwenthllyan Letitia, called from an early age Tickie. She had been born in Victoria in 1899 but because of the war had not been, like her sisters, to school for a period in Germany. She had, however, lodged in Paris after the war with some decayed and impoverished aristocrats, a golden time in her memory. My mother grew up in a large house in a respectable suburb of Victoria called Oak Bay, made of huge blocks of locally hewn granite. It had been designed by the architect Arnold Rattenbury who was eventually, after he had returned to England, murdered by his wife and her lover, their chauffeur. It had a fine garden around it of several acres and then, on the other side of a fairly trivial road, there was a large space of rough land, rising to a peak from which the Pacific Ocean could be observed, known as The Rock. It was eventually bought (perhaps compulsorily) by the municipality in the 1970s.

After a while, presumably not very long, since the *Hood's*

stay at Esquimault cannot have been very protracted, my mother and father got engaged. This must have been about 1921. They married in 1923 and I appeared after an acceptable interval in 1925.

My mother was an extremely nice and kind woman with, as the phrase goes, not an ounce of harm in her. She was not, I have to admit, very intelligent and she was even worse educated but I would not have exchanged her untiring affection, her admirable, very clean cooking or the agreeable things she did with me or enabled me to do for any amount of highbrow conversation. Life became fairly difficult for her after my father's early death in 1935 when her income was much reduced and when, nevertheless, she was determined to secure for me the best possible education.

My first conscious memories are of life in Malta. Our house in Valletta was on the Strada Molini and overlooked the charming Baracca Gardens, which in turn looked down on the Grand Harbour, crowded with the vast grey ships of the Mediterranean fleet. By this time my father was, I think, on the *Barhan*. Our house was very tall and thin but we lived in some style with a very good cook called Borg, some maids and, of course, my Nanny. Nanny Crawford was the person I saw most of in the next few years, until she left to marry a naval petty officer and I progressed to walkers who took me out in the afternoon, rather than gave full time attention. She was a very nice woman and the only real complaint I had to make about her was the insistent clacking of her false teeth (she was in her early twenties) as we shared our meals. These sounds excited extreme nervous stress in me which I still experience in the presence of loud eating noises.

It was in the Baracca Gardens that I did the first bad thing I remember. I had a girlfriend called Mary Rigg whose father was the superintendent of the naval dockyard. She and I were engaged one day in competitive extraction of stones from the pathways of the garden. She came up with an unprecedently large stone that I immediately took from her by force. Nanny observed this and I was taken back indoors and made to sit alone in my room until teatime, reflecting on my moral infirmity. We had some pleasant outings, particularly to the beach at Tini, where I proved better at making sandcastles than at swimming. There were very delightful local rowboats called *dghaisahs*, travel in which gave one an impression of imperial magnificence. At one end of Strada Molini the road ended with a view of the Mediterranean. At the other was Government Street, one of the main thoroughfares of the island, much frequented by the local *carrozzi*, horse-drawn conveyances. One day, walking there with Nanny, a few feet away the horse of one of these carotsi dropped down dead in the street. The driver, realising that it was not going to revive, burst into tears. I was greatly moved by this display of devotion to an animal associate, but I have since wondered whether it was not distress at the loss of a piece of valuable equipment that lay behind his emotional display.

One item I brought away with me from Malta was a beautifully embroidered suiting in which I was photographed, looking rather too good to be true. I must have realised I looked pretty good in it. My father's next posting was to Devonport, near Plymouth, and we lived in a house in Saltash, Cornwall, just over the River Tamar. The house looked perfectly normal from the street side but, on the other side, after a short patch of lawn and garden bed, sank precipitously down to the river which could be reached by a rather dubious stairway. Trips to Devonport and Plymouth from Saltash were either by train over the noble Saltash Bridge or by ferry, which I really preferred. In Plymouth there was the Hoe, where Drake played bowls, and a splendid department store of the kind that used to flourish in English provincial towns in those days. Apart from the normal complement of domestic staff, we had a weekly visit from a Mrs. Bishop who carried out what was rather mysteriously known as 'Heavy Cleaning'. She was a nice woman and particularly interesting to me because of hints my mother dropped about her desperate poverty. She had many children and I rather think that her husband was No Use (no doubt a euphemism for alcoholic). She was a vast woman, of rubicund 18th century appearance.

At this time I started formal education, if that is not too strong a term to describe the pleasant little school run by the two Miss O'Doghertys. One, the taller and more dignified, instructed us in reading and writing, the other, cosier and less authoritarian, led us graciously into the marvels of arithmetic. I fell rather seriously in love with a very pretty girl, somewhat older than I, called Elizabeth Rashleigh. She filled my thoughts at night, but I was far too shy to make any declaration of my feelings.

Not very far away, on the edge of Dartmoor, in Tavistock, lived my great uncle Ernest and my great aunt Bea, in childless comfort. But they were delightfully welcoming to me. He, true to the Indian leanings of my family, had been a tea planter somewhere in the sub-continent, but on early retirement had taken up the post of honorary secretary to the Tavistock Golf Club. The word 'honorary' suggests it was more for occupation than for income. Aunt Bea was a very attractive mature lady, with a powerful air of being an Edwardian Gaiety Girl. I do not for a moment believe she was, but I found her delightful to contemplate. Her teas were massive and excellent.

We must have left Saltash about 1932 when my father went

to a post in the naval metropolis as it then was, of Portsmouth. He went to Haslar, the large naval hospital, first as a doctor and then, at some point which remains unclear to me, as a patient. That meant that he was even less at home than he had been before. In those days people in the navy spent a good deal of time at sea, not commuting to and from offices. What he was suffering from was tuberculosis, contracted from his under-nourished sailor patients. I was never told what was wrong with him. My mother curiously described him as suffering from dysentery. It remains a puzzle why she should have chosen such an unattractive complaint behind which to hide the truth of the matter. It may have been that coming from a family with TB in it I should have been unwelcome at school. This change in my father's status brought about a number of moves.

I came away from Saltash with a little incident in my mind that I have never forgotten. We had a very sweet and charming young maid, who may well have been called Elsie. We were discussing one day in the kitchen what were the worst rude words we knew. My repertoire was very slight at that stage, rising perhaps to '*bum*'. She said she knew some much worse words and I asked her to tell me what they were. First came '*bugger*' whose meaning was not explained and may not have been known to her. But with an air of mounting excitement she said she knew an even worse word than that. I could not persuade her to do more than spell it out, which she did: *F-U-K*.

As a result of my father's move to Portsmouth, it was decided that we should settle somewhere south of Winchester, in a region that already contained my father's parents and his brother Bill. Then in Southsea, next to Portsmouth there was Aunt Sadie, wife of the Admiral who had supplied my father with a letter of introduction to the Jones family in Victoria B.C. and indirectly with a wife. Aunt Sadie was a lively, almost hyper-active person, always jumping up from the table and changing her mind about whatever she had decided a couple of minutes before. I remember her as being exceedingly good looking but I think she must have been a bit of a trial to Uncle Fred who rather hung about in the shadows of the family home. She suffered from a variety of digestive complaints which meant that she hardly ate anything except powders out of fairly large bottles, but she kept a fine table and felt it obligatory to feed me until I threw up, as I occasionally did with her excellent food.

The first place in which we settled, before my father fell ill, was at the end of a lane in my grandparent's village, Twyford. At the top of a lane on the corner of the main road to Southampton was an establishment boldly called the Grocery Shop, run by a modern young couple called the Stansfields. Mrs. Stansfield won my lasting admiration by being able to play the saxophone whose tootling notes one was sometimes able to hear walking down the lane to our house at the end. The other main shop in the village, apart from Dumper's bakery, was just called The Shop. It was run by a tough and heavily made-up old girl called Mrs. Prince. She was not much better than she should have been and cohabited with a rather menacing looking elderly man called the Captain. It was on a very soggy bit of land, pretending to be a village green, on the other side of the road going past my grandparent's house.

I should have mentioned the fact that before we moved into our Twyford dwelling, we stayed for some time in two other places from which more permanent accommodation could be sought. The first of these was the Bridge Hotel in Shawford, which was in fact a pub but claimed hotel status by reason of an aged mil-

itary man, General du Boulay, who had taken up permanent residence there. From there we moved to the Bugle Inn in Twyford
which had even less claim to being a hotel but whose proprietress
firmly referred to it at all times as the Hotel. We finally came to rest
in a house at the far end of a long attractive lane that, in effect, con-
stituted the village of Compton. At the main road end was the village church and vicarage and a string of substantial, professional-
class houses in which lived Cathleen, the beautiful daughter of Dr.
Dominy to whom I was hopelessly enslaved and nearby Azalee, the
daughter of Commander Bake who I now think was in fact the
better-looking of the two. She had a fringe of ruthless geometric
cut and, being mad about horses, tended to wear jodhpurs, or at
least tweed jackets. Cathleen's attire was rather more filmy and
feminine.

I had got to know these girls because of the school to
which I was sent in the nearby village of Shawford. This was called
Down House and was operated by a solid Newcastle lady called
Miss Taylor and her associate, Miss Mays, who was the daughter of
the rather rakish proprietor of a Southampton department store.
He was occasionally visible at the school and I much admired his
square moustache and grey homburg hat. There must have been
about twenty children in the school, some of them boarders, either
by the week or by the term. Some poor souls spent the holidays
there – not that it was in any way unpleasant – because their families were in some far-flung bit of the empire. With three of these
I went for extra mathematics to an old dugout of a schoolmaster
who had been roped in for the purpose. He, poor man, had had a
stroke so that his mouth turned badly down on one side with
intermittent leakage of saliva and dire effects on his audibility. What
with the fascination of the dripping saliva and the slurred utter-

ance, I could make little or nothing of his teaching. I found it particularly hard to master long division. I could aesthetically appreciate the shape of a long division sum, trailing off to the right and attenuating at the bottom, but the logical relation between the numbers entered completely eluded me. Looking at my efforts he protested in his indistinct way, "I cannot see how you arrived at this result." Our class met while everybody else was playing outside. Its other members were Philip Bailey, whose father was, like George Orwell, in the Burma police and two large, brawny red-haired sisters whose parents were in India. These were the members of the school who stayed on during the holidays.

French teaching was in the obviously competent hands of Mlle Bremens, an elegant, austere-looking but extremely amiable French lady, without a trace of makeup and given to severe brown dresses. It did not occur to me to wonder how she had come to be washed up in a Dame school in a small Hampshire village and I am still at a loss about it.

At the end of each week, a small mark sheet would be affixed to the switch on the light in the main schoolroom. There we all were with our work agglutinated into a single figure. The range of marks was often considerable, from 85 say, to 17. Beside each entry was an adjective that summed up the overall performance of the individual pupil. These ranged form the stratospheric heights 'Very Excellent' to 'Poor'. In this none-too-competitive academic atmosphere, I quite often attained the level of 'Very Excellent' and was usually top of the list. My later academic performance, although often quite good, never again reached this altitude.

Towards the end of my time, a year before going away to prep school in 1934, I changed my status to weekly boarder to prepare me for the hardships and deprivations of a boarder's life. We weekly boarders arrived on Monday morning and left or were collected on Friday afternoon. My recollections of Down House are almost uniformly pleasant with one exception. There was a detestable boy called Kenneth Lockerbie, from Miss Taylor's home town of Newcastle, a full boarder. He, by sheer strength of character, compelled me by horrible but unspecific sanctions to do all sorts of things I did not want to do, such as get myself out, while comfortably settled into a game of cricket. The idea was put about that he was not at all well, but he was not ill enough for my comfort.

Early in 1934, my mother and I went on my first trip to her birthplace. This involved crossing the Atlantic in a fairly modest Cunarder, the Ascania, or Alaunia, rather than something larger and more glamorous. On arrival in Montreal I think we must have stayed with another of my mother's aunts, Emily, for a day or two and then we boarded the CPR train for the transcontinental trip. I have done it several times since and it has never failed to be altogether wonderful. The best bit is the furthest west, from Calgary up into the Rockies and then down the other side to Vancouver. From there the final leg is by ferry over the Straits of Juan de Fuca to Victoria.

The household at this quite impressive place – its splendours not suggested by the address: 599 Island Road – consisted of my grandmother, my mother's elder sister Ruth, an intelligent, quite formidable but very agreeable woman and a number of Chinese servants, some indoors, and two in the garden. The senior gardener lived in a romantic little hut at the extremity of the estate. At another extremity was 572 Linkleas Avenue, a neat, quite modern house, which could easily have been in Esher or Virginia Water.

This contained my Aunt Nora, a rather fragile, cultivated lady, and her husband Mick. He had only one leg as a result of service with the Flying Corps in the First World War and hopped around on a crutch. Because of Nora's asthma, they spent winters in Arizona. I was very fond of the senior Chinese servant, the cook, and spent a good deal of time in the kitchen talking to him and watching him prepare the meals. Eating has always been a matter of considerable importance to me. After the war, when I went to visit my mother who had settled there to be with her sister, she remarked one day "everything is so difficult these days, now that there are no more Chinamen." ('These Days' in my mother's conversation, were always contrasted with 'Days Gone By'). This excellent man had trained one of my aunt's unending sequence of black and white terriers to come into the drawing room at dinner time with a piece of string dangling from a tooth with a bit of paper attached, bearing the message: "Dinner is Served Mrs. Jones."

I had a lovely room at the corner of the first floor looking over The Rock towards the ocean. But the most interesting parts of the house to me were the attic and the library. I think I took over most of the attic while I was staying there except for some adjoining compartments in one corner which were dedicated to my grandmother's manufacture of lavender water, made from the copious crop of lavender in the garden and given to be sold for the Blind, with whose welfare she was much concerned. For the still involved in the process of manufacture, she was required to have a liquor licence and to get it, to her immense disgust, she had to appear in person at the provincial liquor licensing office downtown. The library really deserved its name. My grandfather had been a considerable accumulator of books. He had a great many sets of which I still possess quite a few: a beautiful Ruskin, a complete Walter Scott and a 1911 Britannica on India paper are some of them. When a move a few years ago required me to get rid of many of my books, I let go a seventy-volume set of Voltaire published just before the Revolution. In fact there were only sixty-nine volumes because a displeased Chinese servant had removed one and thrown it away. It was only a volume of correspondence. Staying in the house many years later, in 1965, I set myself up in the attic and got down to writing the book by which I set most store, while our children frolicked about down below. I do not know whether I can date a lifetime's involvement with books to this visit to Victoria in 1934, but from then onwards they got a firm and immovable grip on me.

I went to school at an establishment which I think had been attended by my mother and her sisters at an early stage of its history. By my time Miss Ashworth's, which may have acquired a more impersonal name, was a large and flourishing enterprise. A lingering recollection of the words and tune of 'O Canada' and of 'The Maple Leaf Forever' are my most conscious reminders of the instruction I received. More exciting were visits to The Crystal Gardens just behind the Empress Hotel where I went to the swimming pool and did not really learn to swim, and to the ice rink and did learn to skate. I also went to Carley's riding stables where Mrs. Carley, a very convincing Western girl, taught me to ride with the assistance of Piper, an extremely docile retired police horse. He was ideal for a timid rider. I mastered all the ordinary movements, although I did not much like galloping and was a very reluctant jumper, which suited Piper. At weekends we pulled ourselves together and with great baskets of food and drink drove the 15 miles to Metchosin, a delightful property my grandfather had bought a bit further up the west coast of the Island. There were two houses: the main house which was kept for family visits and the lower house nearer the ocean which was inhabited by an extremely large jolly family of Poles who practised some form of primitive agriculture without marked success and were really there to act as caretakers. On these visits I played a somewhat non-functional but frequently photographed part in the activities of the place. At the upper extremity of the property, running along beside the Kangaroo Road, was a railway line for logging purposes. It was still running in those days and I loved to watch the trains go by, like any normal human being.

In the year of my first visit to Canada my grandfather died in his mid-eighties and other disturbing things were going on as a result of my father's transformation from doctor to patient at the Haslar hospital. I was sent over to Twyford to stay with my grandmother. Despite the sad nature of what was going on, I do not remember being notably upset by it although naturally I was cast down by my father's death in 1935. I had always been extremely fond of him but, because of the nature of naval life in those days, I had seen surprisingly little of him. He was a very popular figure amongst his colleagues and the house was frequently full of them. The submariners were the most long-suffering and courteous because of the nature of their work, comparable to that of the cooks in a short order restaurant. The Fleet Air Arm people were the most glamorous: that may be one of the reasons why I went into the air force. Some of my father's popularity must have been due to the fact that he was extremely funny. Unfortunately I can remember little detail of this. He taught me a short poem: "Beans, Beans, the musical fruit; the more you eat the more you toot." I had not grasped the precise meaning of this gem, supposing that the reference was to the high spirits engendered by the consumption of beans. I once recited it to a collection of people my parents had for Sunday lunch. I think it went down quite well, but my mother was very discomfited. But then she was used to that. She was the perfect foil to my father's incessant jollifications. I remember once sitting with him, listening to Rachmaninoff's second piano concerto on the wireless. He used this turbulent work as background to a magnificent piece of mime in which he pretended to be a man in a wheelchair pursued by cavalry or some such menacing force. I thought I was going to be sick and implored him to stop. But he was implacable. He was a great admirer of the writings of Beachcomber, which he bought in hardback form as soon as they came out, having probably read them before in the columns of the *Express*. I continued the collection and have them and love them still. A friend of mine called Joy, the daughter of a former shipmate, once told me that people were still laughing many years after at my father's jokes.

CHAPTER TWO
WEST HILL

Frith and Tony

I had already, in the autumn of 1934, before my father's death, enrolled at West Hill Park, a prep school at Titchfield, a village in Hampshire not very far from the Solent. The headmaster was Mr. C.H. Ransome, an upstanding old blighter whose white moustache was often stained by tobacco smoke. He was distinguished by the fact that he, with a fellow batsman, held the record for a first-wicket stand in non-first class cricket (he played for Free Foresters). He taught Latin but was more memorably responsible for Bible study with which we began lessons for a quarter of an hour each day. This was confined to the New Testament of whose earlier books I still know far more than is necessary. The Old Testament was handled in an enjoyable hour – it being such a splendid book – on Sunday mornings before we trooped down the hill to the village church in Titchfield. Mr. Ransome, or 'The Ranter' as he was more commonly known, had a colourful turn of phrase. I seem to remember he once described Judas Iscariot as "the most frightful bounder," and also indulged in a certain freedom of textual interpretation though I have been reliably told that it was not he who said "you boys have got to remember that in Jesus's time a carpenter was pretty much a professional man," but it was very much in his style.

There were four other masters. The senior of these was Mr. Canham, a noble relic of late Victorian enlightenment. He could have been one of H.G. Wells's earlier heroes in his twilight years. He exuded confidence in science and progress. He soon sorted me out in the matter of long division and, as it turned out, made me quite a good mathematician until my last year in the school when he went quietly mad. He spent all his time in class interrogating us about the erotic games we got up to with each other, a suspicion which was almost wholly devoid of foundation. He used to take us, during the summer term, down to bathe at a neighbouring beach. The trip was accomplished in a former WW1 ambulance whose Red Cross was clearly visible on its side. Once at the beach we all got into our trunks but Mr. Canham emerged from the ambulance we had vacated in an all-enveloping swimming garment round the middle of which, roughly speaking, a very large leather belt was placed. "You'll be wondering what this belt is. This is my appendix belt." No other explanation was forthcoming. If he failed to wear it, would his bowels gush out, as had those of the bounder Judas Iscariot? Mr. Canham had a very large corporation, which led us to an interesting burst of theory. He had a son, not natural but adopted, a rather rough lad who was training to be an officer in the Merchant Navy. We wondered if Mr. Canham's rather abnormal shape might have made it impossible for him to Get It In.

The other masters can be taken as a group: Mr. Armstrong, a sensible man not unlike Des O'Connor in appearance; Mr. Jimmy, who was the headmaster's son, a large handsome young man, and Mr. Bond, the exceedingly good-looking son of a former master of Magdalene College, Cambridge, who was happily paired with an exceedingly good looking wife. This may have compensated for his somewhat lowly position in the education system as compared with that of his father. It occurred to me that it would surely be a good idea for Steve Armstrong and Jimmy Ransome, both bachelors, to marry Miss Cooper and Miss Pile, the two unmarried matrons. I put this suggestion to one of the men one day and was surprised at the difficulty he had to contain his laughter. With the passage of time I came to realise that their sights were set on fresher game than Miss Cooper and Miss Pile. Miss Cooper was a rather grim-looking person who failed to conceal a large lump on her forehead by carefully arranging her hair, and Miss Pile was a thin bespectacled lady apparently permanently twenty-nine years of age who gave off a rather musty smell.

West Hill was an attractive place. It had been a country house until shortly after the war. The grounds were large and varied, not wholly given over to sports pitches and the like, and surrounded by a foliage covered pathway in which it was delightful to walk. The Ranter had his favourites whom he used to address as "dear thing." I did not at all mind not being in this class. Most of them were good at cricket, not very clever and went to Malvern next where the Ranter had some push.

The only serious defect of the school, as I saw it then and as I think of it now, was the food, which was unspeakably bad. The official explanation of this was that Mrs. Ransome, a cultivated lady who kept herself to herself, was delicate, which I presume to be a euphemism for lazy. She did, however, come to my rescue in the matter of a form prize. When I made this application I was in some disfavour with Mr. Ransome for spreading bad language in the school. Some boys in the course of a spot of larking about had pointed imaginary machine guns at each other with the cry: "Bugger, bugger, bugger on the Western Front." I had been away on the day the headmaster instituted enquiries of which the NKVD would have been proud, into the source of this linguistic atrocity. So the accused implicated me, as a convenient Trotsky figure and when I got back to school at the end of my day out I was told that the headmaster wished to see me. After accusing me of spreading filth through the school, he asked me what the word 'bugger' meant. Blushing and looking at the ceiling I said, "I think it is someone whose parents are not married." To his great credit the headmaster, I observed, seemed to be having some difficulty in suppressing his laughter. This incident, nevertheless, made me an object of suspicion. When I asked to have *Anna Karenina* as my form prize, I was met with the stern remark "I suppose that is some of the foreign muck you like." Next day I ran into him in the hall and he said, "Look here, old man, I've had a word with my wife who is a great reader about that book you wanted and she said you must certainly have it because it is one of the greatest books in the world." I thought, and still think, that that was quite impressive.

At West Hill I made my first real friend, as contrasted with the forgettable playmates of an earlier period. Jeremy Johnston and I were both sons of naval captains, both fairly bright, both destined for the naval college of Dartmouth. We used to design imaginary countries together: he designed the military uniforms; I set out the hierarchical table of military and political organisation. He liked to design car bodies of a sort that were frequently met with in *The Illustrated London News* and in what was probably a premonition of his adult life, ball dresses for ladies. As Dartmouth drew near for both of us, he became less and less enchanted with the prospect, while I remained entirely keen. But his peppery father would not hear of a change and off to Dartmouth he went. He survived the war in one piece and I remember going to visit his destroyer which was moored in Portsmouth just after the war to give its crew some leave. He was left behind as officer on duty with a couple of marines as guards and a cook. I think we had an excellent meal, but since the pink gins we drank cost him only two pence a go, I had no difficulty in following his suggestion to make a beast of myself. After long struggles with the Admiralty, he was finally let out of the navy and went on to work for British Olivetti, seduced perhaps by the beauty of their typewriter design. The last time I saw him, a little before his early death, he was living under the thumb of a rather sinister young Frenchman.

Early in 1938 I had my tonsils taken out, in accordance with one of the futile medical fads of the period. Happily I was not subjected to an appendectomy or a mastoid operation, as the great majority of my contemporaries seemed to have been. It may have been the removal of my tonsils that exposed me in the summer of 1938 to pneumonia that proceeded to degenerate into empyema. That involved an operation at the back of my rib cage and the removal of a rib to let out the accumulated pus. An excellent surgeon, Mr. Troup, did this but was out of action with blood poisoning, not caught from me, when a second such drainage was necessary. I spent thirteen far-from-unhappy weeks in the Enniskerry Nursing Home on Sleeper's Hill in Winchester.

CHAPTER TWO: TONY

Why this experience was not so bad was the excellence with which things were managed in the nursing home. It was run by a trinity of wonderful ladies: Miss Bowe from Ireland who was the boss, Sister Askew from England who was the matron in appropriate cap and outfit, and Miss Moffatt, a Scottish lady who, with memorable skill, ruled the kitchen. In the early stages of my long recovery I ate very little, but as I got better, my appetite returned, seemingly invigorated by its long rest. I ate enormously and splendidly: there was no such thing as portion control at Enniskerry. The question "How many sausages would you like?" was a genuine one and I came to answer it with large numbers. The ladies of Enniskerry were quite wonderful and my gratitude to them is boundless. I had my ups and downs during this long stay, inducing Joy, a girl I have mentioned before, to make the statement, "I wish Tony would get better, or something."

For the next stage of my convalescence, my mother and I went for a long visit to the fine house of Aunt Dorothy and Uncle Jack near the Dowlands landslip in Dorset, not far from Lyme Regis. He had settled down to various harmless public activities, which he tended to represent as comparable to the labours of Sisyphus, and more extensively to sailing his boat, the Sam Tully, a twenty-two foot schooner berthed at Lyme. The ship's company when we went out with her consisted of Uncle Jack, his sons Toby and Pat and me and Na, the boy's former nanny whom I was in the habit of referring to as Nurse. She had been kept on in the family as a kind of major domo and took part in everything. One day we were out in the Sam Tully in rather choppy weather and I began to feel distinctly queasy. "If you are going to be sick," said my uncle, "do stick your head over the side." "I think I'll be all right," I said, "If I could just have one of those cream buns I saw being packed." This unusual therapy worked perfectly and I sailed onto the waves unscathed.

I had been intending to present myself that year for the Dartmouth examination but in view of my illness, the admirals, or whoever it was who decided these things, said I was obviously not well enough to go to Dartmouth and suggested that I try what was known as the Public School Entrance at the end of the next stage of my education. This posed the problem of where I was to go next since I was already thirteen. Winchester was ruled out, partly because of expense but also partly because of its unhealthy situation in the marshes beside the river Itchen. In my time it was widely believed among schoolboys that *tinea cruris*, that scourge of public school life, was particularly endemic at Winchester. The decision was made to send me to Stowe in the healthy depths of the Buckinghamshire countryside. The Ranter's idea for my adult career was that I should go into the Sudan Civil Service. But perhaps he was joking. Stowe turned out to be a very good idea for my health, my happiness and my general educational advancement, not to mention what it did for my taste, given the great beauty of the house itself and of the large grounds in which it was set. I have always thought that an education at Stowe is calculated to turn any reasonably sensitive young person into an eighteenth century duke. In the autumn of 1938 I was well enough to go back to West Hill for a final year in which I was, by becoming fourteen in the course of it, a somewhat antediluvian relic of the past.

After the death of my father, my mother and I moved into Winchester from our sequence of more or less rustic homes in Twyford and Compton. We moved into Hyde Abbey, which was not quite what it sounds, being a decent eighteenth century house of which we occupied the first floor. It was not far from the middle of town, being at the end of Hyde Street, the other end of which led into Jewry Street, Winchester's equivalent to Holborn. I was reasonably helpful to my mother about the house, doing a good deal of the shopping. There was a small but richly equipped general store up near the other end of Hyde Street from which I bought a multitude of things including, on every visit, a box of Kup Kakes. These were individual chocolate sponge cakes covered with a fairly thick layer of chocolate and I loved them. We were living in Hyde Abbey for most of the time I was at West Hill. My mother would come down to collect me in her embarrassing Wolseley Hornet, registration number: JY 1170. It cut a rather miserable figure in comparison with the helicopter, or more precisely, autogyro, in which the father of the Cooper brothers, James and Christopher, came once in a while to collect them. I was allowed out for quite a number of Sundays and the effect of the school food was obliterated by the sumptuous feasts, lunch AND tea my mother laid on. My tastes were far from sophisticated. I was particularly fond of roast chicken with bread sauce and two kinds of stuffing, followed by fruit salad and ice cream.

My mother and I made all sorts of outings from Hyde Abbey in the late 1930s. We were often at my grandmother's in Twyford, quite a lot with my aunt Sadie in Southsea and from time to time with some naval friends who had an excellent beach hut at Hayling Island. From time to time I was taken to Southampton to skate with the very pretty Bissett girls, another set of naval offspring, or to go to the only reasonably adventurous restaurant anywhere around, Chez Michel. I imagine the proprietor had at some time jumped ship from a ferry. Around the beginning of the war it moved to Winchester, which was a considerable benefit for discriminating residents. Important buildings for me in the city were the cinemas and libraries, my temples of culture. The cinemas were the Ritz (later Odeon) in North Wall and, a few hundred yards away in Jewry Street, the Royal, a more elderly structure. Seats in the front circle of the Ritz/Odeon were two shillings. There was one other cinema some way further downtown on the edge of a recreation ground. This was made, so far as I could tell, of green corrugated iron. In it for a very modest sum I saw many of the films of Tom Mix and Ken Maynard.

There were also two main libraries of which I made constant use: the City Library on Jewry Street not far from the Royal Cinema and the County Library a little way away just beyond the Odeon. The City Library had formerly been the Corn Exchange and was so described by bus conductors letting one off at the stop there. It was beautifully spacious with the book stacks at decent distances from each other so that no crouching was needed. There was a reference and reading room in which I spent a good deal of time. There was often an oldish man in a kind of monk's attire with a musical score propped up on the desk in front of him and a cardboard version of a piano keyboard on which his fingers rhythmically thumped away. I greatly admired this. The County Library was darker within and much more congested, but its real purpose was not to serve the people of Winchester, although we were welcome to use it and take books out, but rather readers from smaller libraries in the county of Hampshire round about. I had become a fairly serious reader at West Hill. I was first entranced by the rather fustian works of Stanley J. Weyman, such as *Under the Red Robe*. But I was soon led, by whose wonderful advice I cannot now remember, to John Buchan's *Thirty-Nine Steps*. This immediately led me to the rest of the Hannay saga, the Edward Leithen stories and on to Dixon McCunn and also to the start of them all, the incomparable *Prester John*. Funny books occupied a prominent place:

CHAPTER TWO: TONY

Wodehouse, Saki and my grandfather's favourite, Leacock. I have to admit that the great pre-twentieth century giants of literature did not make an appearance until I got to Stowe. But my choice of form prize shows I was not wholly unaware of classical literature.

Two events during our Winchester years deserve attention, both of a ceremonial nature. In 1937 my mother and I went to the Coronation of George VI for which, as a naval widow, she qualified for two admirable seats at the Buckingham Palace end of Constitution Hill. This position provided us with a view of all the important guests as they arrived at the palace to take their places in the procession down the Mall. Then we saw them all again when they came back. It was widely believed at the time that the king disguised his pallid face with pancake makeup. He was of an almost oriental hue on this occasion. In a way, far more exciting to me, was the arrival of Mr. Baldwin, the Prime Minister, in an open carriage. He looked wonderfully like the caricatures I had seen of him. During my time at West Hill I had somehow developed a consuming interest in contemporary British and world politics, purely from a spectatorial point of view and without the least tinge of ideological commitment. I was one of the earlier readers of John Gunther's most enjoyable *Inside Europe* which I approached as a kind of global gossip column, which, to some extent, it was.

Two years later my mother took me to matins at Winchester Cathedral at 11 a.m. on Sunday, 3rd September. The Dean, a man of some grandeur, was looking a little anxious, as well he might, with German troops pouring over Poland's western frontier. We were all waiting to hear whether Chamberlain's demand that they should all go back to Germany was met or whether we were at war. Mrs. Selwyn, the Dean's wife, was walking up and down the aisle while we soldiered on through the lessons and the

Te Deum. A maid, who must have been listening to the wireless, came up and must have reported that the Germans had chosen the second option and the Dean knew which of the two sermons he had prepared he should deliver.

In this connection, some word about my rather vestigial religious life might be appropriate. I have mentioned the biblical studies of West Hill that were agreeable but not very devotional. We often used to go to church in Twyford where my father was buried, and my grandmother a regular member of the congregation. The incumbent, an excellent man, the Rev. Mr. Morris, seemed to believe that it was his inescapable duty to bring Matins to an end well within the hour. He achieved this with extreme fidelity by keeping his sermon exceedingly short. At this time I had a Mickey Mouse watch with a large second hand and I regularly timed him. Four minutes was his maximum, splendid fellow. As this practice shows, I was more a compliant than a devout Christian. The question became pressing later at Stowe when Confirmation loomed. Confirmation classes were conducted by the rather inept Chaplain (there were some quite smart clergy on the staff, but they tended to wear their civilian clothes). He was fair game for embarrassing questions. I realised I did not believe a word of it and was myself somewhat embarrassed by my insincerity in going ahead with Confirmation. Since that time I have not seriously entertained any supernatural beliefs, while acknowledging that if it had not been for Christianity the Dark Ages would have been Dark for much longer, and we should have been deprived of most of our art and architecture and also of a great deal of effective charitable and educational work.

One day, not long after we settled at Hyde Abbey in Winchester, my mother remarked to me that she had made a very nice new friend, a Mrs. Buckley, who had a son who they thought would make a very nice companion for me. When I heard that he was two years younger than I, I rather doubted that he would prove satisfactory in this role. But as it turned out, they were quite right and Jim became one of the best friends I have ever had. He was a person of vast open-heartedness, in no way tainted by ambition or aggressiveness and delightfully ready to laugh paroxysmally at all my jokes, however flaccid. His mother Joyce was a very decent and intelligent woman and his father, a solicitor in Winchester, was in many ways an admirable man. He was very well read and had an excellent collection of books to which I was given access, even to the precious ones which he had had specially bound by Zehnsdorf. Unfortunately, perhaps because of the tedium of life as a Winchester solicitor, he drank far too much and far too often. In due course his marriage came to pieces and he went off with his secretary, a hard-faced but distinctly handsome young woman who kept him in order for the rest of his life.

Jim and I used to mooch around together in Winchester, visiting the green corrugated iron cinema I mentioned earlier, larking about in the adjoining recreation ground, but most of all, pursuing various fantasies into which we imagined ourselves. One of these concerned a family living opposite the Buckleys' house. This place was a rather grand affair and was known to people around as 'Schloss Baring' since a family of the name Baring, of remotely German origin, lived there. Jim and I formed the view that Schloss Baring was the headquarters in Southern England of Nazi military intelligence and that it was our duty, as patriotic British lads, to keep comings and goings at 'Schloss Baring' under close observation. I very much hope the Barings did not suspect any of this.

Not far away there lived a family called Kewley, one child

of which was hopelessly backward and, at thirteen years of age, with her mouth wide open and her head lolling about and with inarticulate sounds emerging, sat in her pram with nanny at hand. One day we ran across them in the street and Nanny Kewley addressed Jim whom she knew slightly, "Oh Master Jim," she said quite correctly, "what a fine big strong man you have grown into," then after a pause she continued, looking attentively at her charge, "my little Nancy will never grow up."

Later in the month of September 1939, in the dreadful JY 1170 my mother drove me down to start at Stowe. My first dormitory occupied the area behind one of the big colonnades on the North Front and must have contained up to twenty boys. At one end there was a communal bathroom with four baths. If the dormitory looked like the sort of Crimean fever hospital served by Florence Nightingale, with half-dressed people lolling about all over the place, the bathroom was more reminiscent of Ingres, with his Odalisques replaced by adolescent boys. There was a certain amount of soap-throwing and towel-flicking but well this side of complete anarchy. Stowe, in my time and I hope since, was always a humane school, some might even say soft. That suited me very well.

Several of the Houses, including mine, had their own dining room. At the end of my first day I trooped into it with the rest and, with vivid memories of the cuisine of West Hill, gritted my teeth in a manly fashion at what was presumably about to be served. To my amazement it was delicious and I had a second helping of the pudding which was a cake made out of Green's Sponge Mixture and saturated with beautifully thick chocolate sauce. As I licked the last bits of the sauce from my lips, I leant back and said, "That was really very good indeed," the looks of horror on the faces of my schoolmates at this gross betrayal of a schoolboy's code of honour in regard to school meals, as if a member of the politburo had said, "Stalin is an ugly fool," was not easily forgettable. Eventually I moved to charming smaller dormitories with beautiful William Morris wallpaper and at most six, frequently four, people in them.

The housemaster of Temple House was Mr. Capel Cure, a dry modern linguist who had been brought to the school by its great charismatic headmaster, J.F. Roxburgh, under whom he had served previously at Lancing. I did not like him very much, but then he did not like me very much, a book-loving swot never anxious to get out on to the playing field. Capel had some slightly questionable habits. He would go round the dormitories in the evening when we were undressing, smelling rather strongly of whisky. But to be fair, I know nothing of anything worse than this.

My view of Roxburgh was very favourable. I loved his immensely courtly manner, the well-cut suits that gave him the appearance of an extremely successful Edinburgh gynaecologist, his practice of addressing everybody as "my dear fellow," his resonant and highly imitable voice and not least, his continuous and serious concern for the welfare of every one of us. He taught every form in the school for one period a week (there must have been fifteen of them). I particularly remember a term spent on the poems of Catullus. He would come into the classroom, not too punctually, so that we had time to settle down, bearing a battered attaché case that he would then open. Inside were a number of hard-worn copies of Catullus that he proceeded to fling around the room, roughly in the direction of the members of the class. His style of translation was a little archaic. To some youthful translator who came up with something like, "you are very beautiful," he would protest with a strangled cry and the words, "My dear fellow, this is poetry, 'thou art peerlessly lovely.'" I am sure he did a lot for us all in the way of improving our manners. Because he was so decent to us we did not want to let him down by our natural barbarity. But what he most consciously wanted to do was to instil some taste. For this, Stowe provided an ideal background. A lot of it the work of Vanbrugh, it is one of the most noble ducal houses, without the heaviness, for example, of Blenheim. He set up and ran a society called the Vitruvian Society for the appreciation of architecture. Everyone, whether they were taking music or not, went to a weekly class with Mr. Snowden, the senior music master, in Musical Appreciation, leading to nothing in the way of tests or qualifications. There was an art school, a fairly hideous inter-war modernistic cube but very well equipped and very well staffed by the Watts, a highly civilised Canadian couple.

And then, for my purposes, there was the Library, an extraordinarily handsome room, not diverted from its former ducal employment. It was filled with large and comfortable leather armchairs that made reading even more pleasant than it was anyway. My house matron was a Miss Dykes, a very round Scottish lady of great warmth of character. She was always willing to indulge my recurrent bouts of hypochondria by giving me a chit to get off games. The time thus released I spent valuably sitting at right angles to the normal position in a Library armchair. At some fairly early point in my Stowe years, I read Thomas Hardy's *Tess of the D'Urbervilles*. I went straight on to *The Return of the Native*, *The Woodlanders* and *Far from the Madding Crowd* and before a year was up I had been through his complete works, not omitting *A Laodicean* and *Life's Little Ironies*. He was the first major author whose complete works I read. For most of my time at school, the

Library was run by a somewhat rascally but attractive master called John Davenport. He was one of several masters who would never have been in the place had it not been for the war. With his conversational allusions to Cyril (i.e. Connolly), Stephen (Spender), Dylan (Thomas) and the like, he brought in a powerful scent of the intellectual *monde*. He always said he was going to ask 'Siwwil' or some such person to come down to Stowe but they never came. His purchases for the Library were not at all stodgy. There was a handsome edition of Kierkegaard's *Journal* that, even in translation, was not exactly schoolboy fare.

But for all his failure to bring literary stars to the school in the flesh, John Davenport was an inspirational figure. He aroused my enthusiasm for the British and American literature of the inter-war years, above all for Auden and George Orwell. From the second of these I acquired some political opinions in a highly filtered state; they might best be described as parlour Trotskyism. As to Auden and Co., I soon became a subscriber to *Horizon* and, through acquiring some missing back numbers, got together a complete set.

CHAPTER THREE
AN EPISODE IN THE ATLANTIC

Tickie and Tony circa 1940

After the war had broken out, my grandmother in Canada began bombarding my mother with proposals that she and I should go and sit the war out in Western Canada where there was plenty of everything and a large, barely occupied house. "You are neither of you any use to the war effort, just two more mouths to be fed" as she imperiously put it. My mother did not want to go, having had enough in earlier life of her mother's thumb. The onset of serious fighting in the West may have concentrated her mind. At any rate, we secured a passage for September on *The City of Benares* sailing from Liverpool to Montreal. Notice was given at Stowe, Hyde Abbey was closed down and its contents stored and, when the day approached, we set off for Liverpool, spending the night of our arrival there in the Adelphi Hotel. I was much impressed by the place, having been little in hotels before with the exception of the almost equally impressive Welbeck Hotel in London where I had once stayed for a few days to go to the zoo, pantomime and so forth with my parents. I had been astounded by the size and complexity of the bill presented to my father as we departed, which he took in the calmest imaginable way.

The following morning we embarked but were told that we should not be sailing for a couple of days since German mines had been dropped in the Mersey and needed to be removed. So two days later we sailed away. We were in a convoy of some twenty ships with destroyer escort and travelled at a miserable 8 knots, the speed of the slowest ship. Quite soon our destroyers left us, much earlier than intended. The two days spent on the minesweeping had brought them to another engagement. So on we went, still at 8 knots. On the third night out, some 600 miles to the west, I was sitting in the first class lounge reading a historical novel about Napoleon. At about 10 p.m. there was a loud bang, the ship shuddered and a cloud of dust rose up from the carpets because of the impact. We had been torpedoed. Since we were on a northerly course, we went to our cabin to get heavy coats and my mother put some essential items – passports, jewellery etc. – into her large handbag. We then returned to our assembly point. For a while nothing happened. Then a man of strongly marked features and a generally authoritative bearing – whom my mother and I between us called Mr. Rogers because it seemed appropriate, but was in fact Colonel Baldwin-Webb, M.P. for The Wrekin – said, "Nobody seems to be coming for us; I think we had better go to our boat station." We did, and arriving there found our boat just about to depart, filled to the brim with Lascars (The City of Benares was the Ellerman Line's leading ship on the London to Bombay route in peacetime). The Lascars did not obstruct our entry and the lifeboat was lowered. Halfway through this process, one of the people lowering it must have run away from his post, or possibly a rope broke. Whatever the cause, the lifeboat dangled from its other rope and nearly everybody in it, including me, fell out into the sea. I tried to hold myself in and could have done so had I not been at the end of the lifeboat nearest the water. A very large elderly lady, previously in front and now above me, fell back on to me, doing nothing to keep herself in. On the way down I was hit on the head by some piece of nautical gear and entered the water in a stunned condition. Coming to, I knew not how far under the surface, I thought to myself I had better get things over as quickly as I could and began to gulp in water. Instants later I was in the open air; I had forgotten that I was wearing, as we were all required to do, a reliable Board of Trade life jacket. A remarkable scene was visible. The ship was tilted up at about 45 degrees with all its lights on and the surface of the ocean was covered with lifeboats, rafts and various kinds of debris. Among them some palm trees in wooden tubs from the lounge were bouncing about.

At the time the lifeboat left the ship's side there must have been something like 60 people in it. By the time it righted itself in the water there were about 20. One of them was my mother, still with her handbag, who had somehow moved from the bow to the stern of the lifeboat. By the weird light of the ship, she saw me flailing about and called as loudly as I have ever heard her, for me to swim to her. My very primordial breaststroke sufficed for me to get to the boat where she helped me in. This was made easier by the fact that the boat was completely waterlogged, with only the bow and stern sticking out of the water. When I had time to reflect, this did not worry me, since as a keen student of nautical matters (I had asked for and been given *Jane's Fighting Ships* for Christmas in 1936) I was confident that the regulation requiring lifeboats to carry buoyancy tanks had been observed. We looked around in the water trying to encourage individual swimmers to join us in the boat. Among them was Colonel Baldwin Webb to whom we were indebted for our present somewhat marginal degree of security. He was striking out into the darkness and gave us a cheery wave, clearly unaware of the Board of Trade regulation in which I had so much confidence. He was never seen again and in due course a by-election was held.

Of the 20 people left in the boat, there must have been about equal numbers of passengers and Indian crew. It was cold and stormy and a good many passengers and all but three of the crew members died in the following twenty hours. The passengers who died were mainly elderly or very young, including two of the unaccompanied urban children who were being evacuated to the safety of Canada. These deaths were not unpleasant to see or, so far as I could tell, to suffer. Those who died just sank quietly into unconsciousness. Their bodies floating about in the boat presented something of a problem. A wordless agreement between the most enterprising of the Lascars – known to me and my mother as Gunga Din – and me enrolled us as an informal burial party. We gently eased the dead over the side after a fair pause to ensure that they really were dead. A further implicit understanding between Gunga Din and me was that we should not throw anyone over until any relative they had in the lifeboat was dead too. An example was an elderly Dutch Jewish couple. The old wife died first and her husband rocked her to and fro in the water in front of him, a scene made more poignant by the fact that the old lady's wig had become detached.

It was a cold night and the next day was cold too. We went up and down on vast waves as if in some amusement park, and in the course of these ups and downs had momentary views of other lifeboats in similarly helpless conditions. Not long after we took to the boats we saw one boat which was in magnificent, regatta-like order, with oars in place and everyone seated in an orderly fashion, singing 'Oh God Our Help in Ages Past' and making firmly away from the wreck. They were not seen for another ten days, but were finally picked up in moderately good shape. Often I managed to get the water round me reasonably warm but then a wave would crash on to the boat and my little warmed up region would be replaced by cold sea. Gunga Din found a crate of cans of sweetened condensed milk around our feet. We opened the tins with a rowlock and handed them round. It was all there was, but it was pretty good all the same. After day broke, members of our ever-diminishing ship's company began to see hallucinatory rescue vessels in the distance. After a bit of this, I felt my spirits sink and believed we were all done for. Then at about 2 in the afternoon, an entirely material destroyer appeared not too far away, and a little while later a rowboat from it passed near us. The man in charge of this shouted as they went by, "We are just picking up people on rafts and so forth, we'll be back for you later." The afternoon was long but not devoid of hope except for one of our number, Mr. Ernest Szekulas, a publisher from Hungary, who loudly asserted after a while, "They have forgotten us, they will never come." My mother would have none of this. Falling back on pidgin English for this particular exchange, she loudly affirmed "Big ship come!" and so it did, at about 6. Sailors jumped into our boat with ropes, which they tied round the waists of the more infirm who were then hauled up on board while the younger and more active mounted on rope ladders. There were eight of us left: my mother and I, Mr. Szekulas, a northern-looking man we baptised J.B. Priestley who sat throughout our boat ride with a cap on his head and an empty pipe in his mouth, and an unfortunate woman, a daughter of Thomas Mann, whose two children had died in the boat and whose husband had never made it, and three Indians: Gunga Din, Basil Rathbone and Old Mother Riley.

The destroyer that rescued us was the HMS Hurricane. The captain aimed it at Greenock and we sailed at full speed, carving through the waves at something like 40 knots. It was very nice on board. By judging things correctly I could get each meal twice, once in the fore part of the ship and once in the stern. The privations of the previous twenty hours were soon made good. One rather glorious fact: my mother gave her considerable bundle of sodden money to a sailor to be dried out in the ship's engine room. Her confidence was not misplaced; it all came back, nice and dry. We landed at Gourock (for Greenock) to find the unfortunate Mr. Geoffrey Shakespeare, the minister responsible for the evacuation scheme, to greet us in an appropriately mournful fashion. At first it was thought that 99 children had been lost. But that did not take account of those in the well-found lifeboat we had seen sailing away, which somewhat reduced the toll. We were taken into Glasgow and put up in some style in the Central Hotel, my mother proudly wearing the shoes with which Greenock public assistance had replaced those she had lost in the lifeboat. As we registered, a respectable-looking man with a neatly trimmed beard identified himself as L. Marsland Gander of The Daily Telegraph, somewhat stressed by the thought that other correspondents had got all the best materials for their fabrications already. His article, when it appeared the next day, displeased my mother by crediting her with the somewhat over-ripe formula "through the gathering dusk a destroyer was discernible..." I was quite happy to have myself described as "the sturdy 15-year-old son of Mrs. Quintan, a Winchester lady," not at all upset by the misspelling and grateful for the somewhat euphemistic 'sturdy.'

Next morning we took the train for Euston, and an air raid being in progress, decided to stay at the Euston Hotel. There were no rooms available, but the management kindly allowed us to sleep in the lounge where, as the air raid progressed, cracks appeared in the plaster of the ceiling and powder fell from them. In the morning we hailed a taxi outside the hotel and asked to be taken to Waterloo. The taxi driver told us that the track west of Waterloo had been bombed but that trains for the southwest were running from Clapham Junction. We took his advice and were soon on our way to Winchester, where another taxi took us to Twyford and my grandmother's house.

We pushed open the gates to find my grandmother a little way off on the drive, bent double, weeding. This unusual task had not improved her temper and she stood up and with some asperity said, "Oh, so you're back, are you?" I felt at the time that with this kind of sang-froid we were not going to lose the war.

CHAPTER FOUR
BACK IN ENGLAND

Back in England

My grandmother's house was, I am sorry to say, called 'Clevedale' and was slightly more of an establishment than this name suggests. We carried on here, contentedly, for some time with my mother away at her war work, helping to run catering at a neighbouring airfield and I mainly back at Stowe, where I was reabsorbed without a murmur, having missed only a few weeks of term. Also in the establishment were Mrs. Cox, an ancient slattern, who described herself grandly as "cook-'ousekeeper up to Mrs. Quinton's" and showed equal grandness in the dinners she served, for which the table was elaborately laid and which consisted of soup, usually Bovril, a main dish – shepherd's pie say, or rissoles – a pudding such as plums and custard, and then, with special ornamental plates and cutlery with mother of pearl handles, dessert, a wartime minimum of a couple of apples and a pear. "Shall I clear the dessert now Mum?" she would say at the close of the festivities. There was also a rapidly changing succession of heavily made-up, man-obsessed maids or "girls." In the garden there was Mr. Drew, an almost perfect instance of a gardener, taciturn, hard working, a bit mysterious. My Winchester life was not in the least abridged. Two excellent bus services – King Alfred and Hants and Dorset – took one there for fourpence. My mother had a slight and wholly irrational preference for the former. I was more easy-going.

This went on until my grandmother's death, after a happily short illness, in 1942. In the circumstances the administration of her funeral fell to me. I arranged for her to be buried by her husband in Twyford churchyard. I dealt with all the questions raised by the very competent funeral director: nature and fittings of the coffin, lined but not too extravagantly with some seemly fabric, and fitted with elegant but not showy handles. We sent out the news in all directions and I arranged for flowers. I had in no way been trained for this work and I was quietly satisfied with the efficient way in which I had carried it out. I think my grandmother would have been pleased by the absence of fuss and fidgeting. My grandmother's death entailed another move. So we transferred to the hospitality of Mrs. Samways, who supplied room and board in a fair-sized house half a mile away. The house was called 'Kilravock,' a word whose pronunciation is made clear by a framed poem of thanks by a previous resident:

> *Oh, how can I worthily sing of Kilravock,*
> *With its generous chatter and gay kindly talk?*
> *For now at the moment of saying goodbye*

Salt tears are bedewing my right (and left) eye.
The ignorant Sassenach calls it Kilravock
And makes of its name unbelievable havoc,
But whether Kilravock or whether Kilrork,
Nowhere else shall I ply such a good knife and fork.

Mrs. Samways was an active, stringy old bird, the widow of the District Drainage Supervisor of the Borough of Weymouth. Closely associated with her was her devoted companion Miss Stone, known except in very formal moments as "Dinks." She had an independent career as the local Spirella representative, a corsetière working from door to door. We were not here long but it was quite memorable. The place was spacious enough for me to have Jack Manley, the first close friend I made at Stowe, to stay. It was very much his cup of strong tea. His real name was John but the poetic distraction of his surname impelled me to call him Jack. He was a very straightforward British boy, honest, good at games, but what particularly appealed to me was an outstanding sense of the ridiculous. Once, staying with him at his family's curious little wooden house in Paignton, Devon, when they were out one night and we were dealing with the last remnants of our supper, he let out a hoarse cry and disappeared into the garden, reappearing at the window, his face hideously distorted, crying out "It's the Krit, the Krit, it's come over me again!" and with this, sinking back into the darkness outside. He continued to suffer from the ravages of this imaginary Oriental disease, worthy of Conrad, for some minutes, making it possible for me to compose myself again. Jack was my first study-mate and we shared until prefectorial promotion led him into a study of his own. During our cohabitation we developed a practice of serving absolutely enormous teas to our friends and ourselves (although the Stowe cuisine was good, it still left room for this kind of thing).

I once played a rather unkind trick on him. There was a lively but exceedingly unattractive music teacher at the school called Iona Radice. Her father, like Mrs. Samway's, was also in the sanitary field, but the drains for which he was responsible were those of Calcutta, a more daunting responsibility. Every year she put on a rough and ready comedy in which she played the female lead and dragooned some boy for the male role opposite her. The text required the hero to smother the face of the heroine with passionate kisses. I got wind of this and firmly declined to play the part, suggesting Jack as a much more plausible alternative. He went into the trap and had to serve Miss Radice's erotic appetite for three nights and goodness knows how many rehearsals.

Our friendship continued at Oxford after the war where he had an extremely small, fuggy room in Hertford where the teas were still as copious. With his outgoing and imaginative nature he should have become a schoolmaster but instead he took on the honey farm of an uncle in the Wallingford area. We used to exchange visits with Jack and his wife (Jill of course) in my teaching years at Oxford. He died in a wonderfully characteristic way. He and Jill were due to go to a vast ball in the Grand Room at Grosvenor House for honey producers or some other group. Shortly before, Jill, who was very serious about her singing, received an invitation to perform in a prominent role which was just too attractive to turn down. She got him to take his young secretary in her place. When the dancing was well under way, Jack said to the girl that he was feeling rather tired and would like to sit down for a bit. They did so: he emitted a groan and died. Apparently the Grosvenor House staff put on a brilliantly unobtrusive performance. The only consolation for the poor girl is that he did not pop off on the floor in mid-waltz.

From the Samways' ménage my mother and I moved to relatively permanent quarters at the more attractive part of the village, to one end of a handsome building called Orchard Close. Our wholly self-contained bit was called Orchard End. Gladys and Doris Richardson, who let it to us, were step-mother and step-daughter. Gladys was curiously like a gypsy fortune teller in slightly reduced circumstances, a nice enough person but a little hard to fathom. Were there great depths there or none at all? She was the widow of Jim Buckley's father's senior partner whose first wife was the mother of Doris. Doris was a gawky, unwieldy sort of woman, wholly devoid of feminine charms but very intelligent and very nice. I soon found good employment in their household exercising their dogs: Don was an elderly and quite dignified Springer spaniel of considerable size and thoroughly sweet natured. He being a big dog although getting on a bit, much enjoyed the very long walks during which I took them over the downs past Morstead to St. Catherine's Hill. Weasel was a dachshund of moderately irritable disposition, although he and I soon developed a close friendship. He was much more intelligent than his massive comrade. We stayed there until I became a fellow of a college in Oxford, at which point my mother moved to a highly respectable part of Earl's Court, not far from the stratospherically High Anglican church of St. Cuthbert's, Philbeach Gardens.

Another close friend I met at Stowe was Frank Tuohy, who had a flat, Irish-looking face, although his father was a GP in Sussex. We did not get on all that well because he was undoubtedly more intellectually sophisticated than I and looked down on me as a result. However, I was about the best there was to be had in the way of intellectual companionship and, like a mismatched elderly married couple, we rubbed along reasonably well, chattering about Yeats and Malraux and André Breton. He suffered from some obscure heart complaint for which a cure has since been discovered, which meant he was wholly protected from the menace of games and spent the time we were getting covered with mud in fishing in the school's fine lakes. He went on to King's Cambridge where I visited him when I was in the air force in Lincolnshire and where he read English and became even more culturally exigent.

There was one other genuine intellectual in our House whom we regarded with some awe, a mysterious fellow called Martin Shearn (clearly an anglicised spelling of Schön). His taste was so exquisite that he read only half a dozen authors (Chaucer, Shakespeare, Milton, Donne, Hopkins, Eliot). Some of the singularity of his character may be explained by the fact, which he recounted to us, that rootling about in the family home, he had come upon his step-father's very explicit love letters to his mother. The most interesting friend was John Simopoulos, whom God preserve, I am glad to say, a Greek as may be inferred, whose father was Greek Ambassador to Britain. The embassy, like the Greek Royal family, spent the war years in Claridge's. When I visited the Causerie with John many years later, the waiters addressed him as "Master John." He was, and happily still is, a splendidly eccentric figure. To give an example, David Luke, an Oxford friend of ours, the distinguished translator of Goethe and Thomas Mann, had a childish, immature appearance, did not shave, as was shown by long sparse whiskers dangling from his chin and spoke in a high, lady-like voice. Shortly after the war, planning some foreign travel and motivated by a deep-seated Scottish detestation of unnecessary expense, he asked John Simopoulos if he could borrow some of his luggage for the trip. "Yes," said Simopoulos, "as long as I can first have a look at your private parts." I never learnt how this worked out, but he did borrow the luggage.

There were other masters who did something for me apart from John Davenport. There was George Gilling-Lax who taught very early history out of J.H. Breasted's *Ancient Times*. We got to know more about Sumer, Babylon and the Chaldeans than the average British schoolboy. He soon went off to join the air force and won our admiration by dying in a Mosquito, that most beautiful of warplanes. Roy Meldrum, of the Cambridge education department, a tall rather lugubrious but still entirely amiable Leavisite, taught English with much more intellectual austerity than G. Wilson Knight, also washed up at Stowe by the war. Meldrum had a huge, lean dog, very much like himself in appearance and temperament, who used to lie in front of the electric fire during tutorials, yawning. Wilson Knight, who had written some bizarre works of literary criticism and who had a brother enchantingly called Jackson Knight (author of *Roman Virgil*) had wild flying hair and spoke dramatically with a strong trace of an Indian accent. He was not an Indian but we strongly suspected that his mother had been. History was my main subject and by the time I was fairly advanced in this, I was taught by a stolid but competent man called Ben Fawcett. He seemed to be in bounding good health and of military age, but he got no nearer the battlefield than to be commanding officer of the OTC, at whose parades he cut a nobly convincing figure. He had an exceedingly red face while his wife, otherwise a personable woman, was preternaturally pale. I formed the view, which secured widespread acceptance, that he was a vampire, and that when he and Mrs. Fawcett retired to bed they did not engage in the normal activities of married couples in good health in the prime of life, but that he drew back his lips and sank his white teeth into her jugular vein. There was one master, Fawcett's predecessor in command of the Corps, who was completely but harmlessly mad.

I settled back into the school quite well. I told my shipwreck story to anyone who was prepared to listen. (In Twyford people were anxious, or so they said, to hear about our 'Terrible Experience', so that my mother and I came to refer to it as 'the TE': as in, "Mrs. So-and-So is coming round later, she wants to hear about the TE.") I did not suffer anything other than this narrative loquacity as an after-effect of the experience except, according to the testimony of the other boys in my dormitory, that I had a tendency to fits of shouting in my sleep. I had no recollection of accompanying nightmares and sometimes wondered if they had not made it up. Academic work went steadily forward, the consequent promotion to higher forms led to a progressive withdrawal of the demands of games, and so to fewer appeals for Miss Dykes's invaluable chits. Late in 1942 I went up to Oxford to sit for a scholarship exam for a trial run, listing Christ Church, Merton and Oriel as my chosen colleges. I was interviewed by the first and last of these and was eventually awarded a fairly grand scholarship, the St. Cyres, by the first. While staying in Oxford, where John Simopoulos already was, I met a number of people who became good friends and generally enhanced my life. First of these was Borys Chwolès (later Villers to assist the English mouth), a Polish refugee whose father, a flax tycoon, had had the good sense to get out with most of his assets in the late 1930s, and in England successfully took up the manufacture of electric blankets. Borys was by no means handsome; he looked like a bargain version of Victor Mature. This in no way obstructed his amorous career. He was extremely funny and very well read in a somewhat narrow, aesthetic way. He was the centre of a social circle whose spirit was rather far removed from the struggle of the free nations. One member was an ancient gay called Hedley Hope-Nicholson, worthy of William Plomers' fine description: "a rose-red cissy, half as old as time," who was seized by the extravagantly heterosexual Borys one night in the course of a small dance party we were having to the gramophone. He was whirled round the room, the event closing with a passionate kiss on his heavily made-up lips. What the respectable girls from women's colleges and finishing schools made of it all I was probably too elevated to consider or observe. The other main figure in the group, so far as I was concerned, was Euan Graham – a very tall and distinctly handsome Etonian, who had a nice dry wit and tended to talk almost exclusively in Wodehousian English.

The war being what it was, I decided to come up as soon as possible, that is to say, in January 1943. I then passed two terms of almost uninterrupted pleasure, living on such accumulated intellectual capital as I had for my history tutorials with the very distinguished and courteous Keith Feiling and the charming and abstracted Nowell Myres, a leading historian of the Anglo-Saxon period who took me for 'Political Thought.' I relied for this on mother wit and Sabine's invaluable *History of Political Theory*. At the end of this brief period in Oxford I sat two 'sections' and by passing them got two-thirds of the qualification for a shortened wartime BA. It would not have been worth the parchment it was written on. I did go to one or two lectures out of curiosity but not in any persistent way. On coming up, I had read Law for two weeks after quite a tussle with the authorities at Christ Church. A couple of tutorials on Roman Law (manumission and *patria potestas*) together with a bit of Kenny's *Outlines of Criminal Law* whose definition of larceny I still remember, did the trick and I came back to the historical fold. I attended an Eights Week (i.e. supposedly humorous) debate at the Union where I appeared as Dr. Emilyan Serafimovich Boruschka of the twin universities of Zagreb and Split with a beard and wearing heavy black boots and some kind of frock coat. I am quite unable to remember what rubbish I talked but I do recall the dinner beforehand. The pudding was cherry pie and I proceeded, despite the earnest protests of the charming girl next to whom I was sitting, to chew them up, hoping to establish my *bona fides*. I suffered no ill effects.

I had a very beautiful room in Peckwater Quadrangle with two bedrooms and from time to time had people to stay in the second one quite officially. Such were the privations under which we laboured. Local restaurants, with their 5-shilling limit, supplemented the rugged college food. Best of all was the Taj Mahal in Turl Street. For more formal occasions there was the George. But nobody had a car at this time so we did not get out into the surrounding country as we did when I came back in 1946. Every week on Wednesday there was the Air Squadron. At Stowe I found the old-fashioned khaki uniform of the Corps almost unbearably scratchy and had to wear a pair of pyjama legs under my breeches and puttees. I quite enjoyed the mock battles we had, conducting ourselves in rigid adhesion to the formula, "Down, crawl, observe, fire." I lent a little drama to one of these which, as a recently promoted sergeant, I was leading a section and said to them, "All is lost, we are done for – run for your lives!" which was not included in the instruction manual. To overcome scratchiness I decided to join the newly formed Air Training Section, carrying with me my rank of sergeant. For some time we had no uniforms at all but eventually a consignment arrived but it contained no uniform big enough for me. Some time later we were on parade, being inspected by a retired Air Marshall. Coming to me, in my uniquely civilian outfit, he asked why I was not in uniform. I explained and he said he would ensure a large enough uniform would be sent me. Happily he was not as good as his word and the uniform never came. The Air Training Section was a natural avenue of approach to service in the air force when the time came, but scratchiness of army clothing was not the only reason for my preference for the RAF. As someone who four years ago had been hoping to go to Dartmouth, I might have been expected to opt for the Navy. But being rather fat around the middle, I did not fancy myself in the tight fitting rating's uniform I would have to wear until, if ever, I got a commission. I had also heard from an older boy visiting the school that in air-crew one always slept in sheets. This rumour, which did the trick, turned out to be absolutely correct. My entire three years and a bit of war service never saw me sleeping without sheets. If, however, I had been at Cambridge, I might have found it hard to resist qualifying for a hat-band bearing the initials of the Cambridge University Naval Training Section.

CHAPTER FIVE
AIR FORCE

Tony in flying kit

On 21st August 1943, I presented myself at Stockleigh Hall, a block of flats on Prince Albert Road overlooking Regents Park. This had been requisitioned, together with several neighbouring blocks, to accommodate those arriving at the Air Crew Reception Centre for induction into the air force. The week I joined there were 1,863 of us, a record. Various understandable preliminaries to an air force career then took place. One of the more amazing was the mass swimming test and inoculation of us all at the Seymour Hall baths. There we all were, stark naked, a sight I had never seen before and have not since. I passed my swimming test without distinction but comported myself more impressively at the inoculation. This took the form of a surrealistic parody of a fashionable wedding. Still in our birthday suits, we walked in line between two ranks of medical personnel, each holding some sort of syringe with which they sought to protect us against a broad range of maladies. As a veteran invalid and constant recipient of injections, I breezed through this, unlike some of my fellow recruits, several of whom fainted away. One morning we were taken through the mysteries of the equipment – haversacks, kit bags and so forth with which we were about to be supplied. The corporal carrying out this explanation was a youthful Londoner who picked up a mysterious contraption of straps and buckles with the memorable words in his pronounced London accent, "Dis 'ere is der skellington webbin'." I turned to the sensible looking man beside me and, in an undertone said, "Devised of course by the 18th Century sadist, the Marquis of Skellington." I had chosen the right man to confide in. It was Robert Bolt who became, a well-known playwright and we were friends for the rest of his life.

I went on, after a couple of weeks, to Initial Training Wing at Stratford-on-Avon and Robert did so as well. We had a full life of dramatic fantasy together. We had a regular turn of addressing each other as working-class conservatives. "It's against yuman nature, innit" was one of our feigned objections to left-wing policies. "The bank'll never stand for it" was another. He was responsible for further fantasy. At that time a member of the Communist party, he felt obliged to claim a working class parentage. His accent and his having been at Manchester Grammar School counted against this. The matter was finally settled when I went to stay at his home in Sale and met his parents, the owners of a successful furniture shop and suspiciously well-spoken. Our time at ITW was much relieved by incessant visits, whether on or off duty, to the Tudor Dairy where the cakes, despite war-time restrictions, were quite excellent. The initial training, to which the ITW owed the first two letters of its name, was much the sort of thing I had already done at my Air Squadron Wednesdays: aircraft identification, map reading and so forth, and of course, the inevitable drill. At one of these sessions I turned in the wrong direction and was asked by the corporal in charge of the activity "What's the matter with you then?" a question perhaps not really requiring an answer. "War weariness, Sergeant," I replied. "I'll give you war-weariness," he said. The mildness of this rebuke being, no doubt, attributable to my tactful elevation of his rank.

After ITW I went to one Elementary Flying Training School and Bolt to another. At Elmdon, near Birmingham, a very kindly sergeant – a pilot called Webb – tried to teach me to fly. I could take off quite convincingly, climb and then fly straight and level. I even banked with some distinction. Matters deteriorated when it came to landing although my bumpy descents were never attended by major damage to the aeroplane (a Tiger Moth) or anything else. My real failure was in aerobatics, which I loathed and feared. Sometimes we would reach a reasonable height and he would put the plane into a spin, inviting me to bring the plane back to a normal position. I was no good at this at all. In his report he was very kind. He wrote approvingly of my general competence but said I was "a bit nervous about aerobatics." Because of this I was destined to be a navigator, an entirely sensible decision. At the end of the course I had to hang about the station for a while until it was time to go to Manchester, to Heaton Park to be exact, where initially trained air crew were held until a place was available for them on a troop ship to wherever they were going to be trained further. Robert Bolt rejoined me at Heaton Park and we had a fairly high old time. We used to hang about the Long Bar of the Gaumont in Manchester, hoping to pick up girls. We never got very far with this. One night we were accompanied by a fellow cadet, a clergyman's son called Dervis Ward-Pugh. He was much more worldly than we were although he did no better than we did that night. He had a rather unreliable looking moustache, black and thin like that of an Argentinean tango dancer. As we stood in the rain, not uncommon in Manchester, waiting for our bus back to Heaton Park, large black drops began to flow down his chin from his moustache. We drew his attention to this untoward occurrence and with perfect composure he took out, first his handkerchief to wipe away the offending drops, and then a small tin of black unguent, which he applied to the moustache to keep it the right colour. The last I saw of him was many years later in what must have been one of the most inexpensive B pictures ever to emerge from a British studio in which he played the part of a minor gangster in an overlarge overcoat and was allowed one sentence of dialogue. We hung about at Heaton Park, which was used simply for storage, not any kind of training, for several weeks. We then separated, Bolt to train in South Africa, I in Manitoba, Canada.

Number 1 Central Navigation School was at Rivers, a fair train ride, accomplished at most weekends, from Winnipeg. The training involved a great deal of low flying, which I came quite to enjoy, over the prairie where we passed over more or less identical villages, each with three churches: Catholic, Protestant and Orthodox. It was at Rivers that I made my first serious step forward into relations with women. In the mess hall there was one tall and distinctly good-looking girl. I got to know her, found that she was called Phyllis and, with her assistance, advanced further into maturity. I am afraid to say that I took her away from an entirely unsuitable short man called Root or Roots. I cannot get out of my mind the pained look on his face, like that of a kicked dog, when it became clear what way things were going. The nearest town was called Brandon and there I was entertained by a lady (supplied by a welfare officer) of large cultural pretensions but to whom I am grateful for some excellent meals, a charitable role for us exiles. I did have to stifle my somewhat dismissive opinions about the novelists with whom she consoled herself in the remoteness of Manitoba.

At the end of my stay at Rivers, I travelled westward to Victoria for a two week visit to my grandmother. By that time too many people were running away after their period of training in the dominions for them to be granted any leave until they got back to England. My grandmother was in a position to pull some strings on my behalf and an exception was made in my case. I had two lovely weeks at Oak Bay and then headed east to Moncton, New Brunswick where there was a holding camp for people who had been trained in Canada. Because of my two weeks leave in Victoria, I just missed a troop ship back to England. I managed to keep a straight face when an officer commiserated with me for missing the boat. Even then I thought, what I am pretty certain of now, that the delay saved my life. Moncton was a town of limited interest, but it did contain one magnificent facility: the Kent Soda Fountain. The Kent Special, at 75c, was the star item on the menu. It consisted of three large scoops of differently flavoured ice cream, separated from each other by such lubricants as crushed pineapple and marshmallow fluff. The rule was that if you could finish a second one, no charge would be made for it. The first time I tried this I failed, but I trained myself for a second attempt and brought it off. I thought it wiser not to try to repeat the experiment a third time.

I sailed back on the *Mauretania* and, now being an officer, I had much more comfortable accommodation. This was just as well since the ship was crowded, mainly with huge Canadian soldiers making for the front. The date was quite a while after D-Day, September 1944. In this connection I had one of my more terrifying wartime experiences. I was ordered one day to serve as Orderly Officer, going round the mess-halls accompanied by a sergeant who cried out as we entered each of these places: "Orderly Officer, any complaints?" I was not actually assaulted, I suppose they realised I had had no hand in the cooking, but it was a testing event.

After a couple of weeks at home in Twyford I headed for Scone near Perth in Scotland, to become familiar with British flying conditions. It was here that I was put together with some others to make a crew. Our pilot was a hefty, decayed, gentlemanly figure who drank rather a lot. After a couple of outings with him he was, to my relief, sent off to more sedentary work and I acquired the pilot with whom I served for the rest of my time. This was Stanley Milton who came from Hastings where his parents owned a modest hotel. They did not live in it but in an adjoining dwelling, called "Stan-Den-Der" as a tribute to Stan and his brothers, Dennis and Derek. Stan was a remarkably good-looking fellow, much like Gregory Peck but less stupid looking. He was an instance of something I have often met with in startlingly handsome people of both sexes: They show little erotic interest in members of the opposite sex, let alone their own. It is as if their own beauty is sufficient for them. Stan was a deeply serious person but a good friend and, in a way more important, a most gifted pilot. We got on very well despite being very different people. Sometimes we went out on his motorbike, with me holding on to him around the middle as if I were his fiancée. It seemed only right that a pub should be the goal of these high-speed journeys, but when we got there he would order a lemonade. I sought to approximate to his austerity by having a light ale.

Another member of the crew was our rear gunner, Curly Cave. He had been a Barnardo's Boy as a child and spoke with the utmost fondness about what they had done for him. When we went to a pub as a crew and there was a Barnardo's box on the bar as there often was, he would insist that we all should make a contribution. A shilling was acceptable, but sixpence was looked on with disfavour. The co-pilot, an excellent, cheerful, bulky Londoner looked just like his name: Wally Swain. There was something Tudor about him. There were three others: a bomb aimer, a wireless operator and a mid upper gunner. Once we had reached cruising height I, as navigator, was continuously employed, either with fairly primitive spherical trigonometry, tracing directional beams from radio beacons, in the hope that their intersections would all be in one spot, or near it, or when flying at night, which was when our real business would take place, up in the astrodome taking star shots with my sextant and then, after consulting some elaborate tables and seriously hoping that I had got the right star, entering the resulting bearing on my chart. This was hard and uninterrupted work. I somewhat resented the Tahitian idleness that came over everybody else in the crew once we had reached our operating height. The wireless operator turned on the Light Programme, the pilots lolled back in their seats, letting George (the automatic pilot) do the flying. I felt I was really earning the slightly larger salary which I got as the only officer on the plane.

From Perth, where we flew Wellingtons, a decent old family-style bombing plane, we moved to somewhere near Newark to an establishment which seemed at first to have a religious significance, called a Heavy Conversion Unit. Here we learnt to operate in our various ways the most splendid of all British bombing planes, the Lancaster, with its magnificent Rolls Royce engines, a Bentley compared to the Morris saloon of the Wellington. Suitably converted, we moved to our squadron, No. 505, at Lindholme in Lincolnshire, and prepared to unleash ourselves on the Nazi foe. What we were required to do were called diversionary raids. We would set off fairly early in the evening, with no bombs loaded, and make for – shall we say - Stettin, so as to draw the fairly miserable remnants of the German night fighter force in that direction to get them out of the way of the real business of the night which would take place much further south. I have to confess that in these relatively unferocious operations I never saw a German night fighter, although we did encounter a little harmless flak. It might seem that these diversionary raids were rather unsporting in the circumstances. But the Germans had some characteristically mean-spirited tricks still up their sleeve. They used to send long range night fighters – Ju 188s – to hover around air fields at the time the bombing force might be expected to come home and then pick them off as they made their approach. Once detected, this tactic did not last very long. British night fighters were called in to keep the skies clear. The only tricky moment in my time with 505 Squadron was once when we caught fire fairly near home. Smoke billowed up from below. I was scared stiff. I pulled out the lead of my intercom so that any whimpering that might escape me did not bring about a general breakdown of morale. Taking up some floorboards, we soon diagnosed the problem. A broken oil lead was dripping oil on to an exhaust pipe that helped to keep us warm and was ignited by its heat. Either we turned the oil pipe off or the exhausts. Then we got to work in good conscience with the extinguishers provided and came down in good order. As we approached we saw, near the runway, the fire engines and meat wagons (i.e. ambulances), which had been summoned by Stan's report of our difficulties.

VE Day saw the station medical officer inspecting us all to see if we were fit for service in the Far East and saying that we all were. He was totally drunk. However, instead of being hurled into battle against the unspeakable Japanese, we were sent home on Indefinite Leave, being told to be ready for instant recall. As it turned out I was left at home until after the Japanese surrender, to my very great relief. But I was not idle. Soon after I got home, a delightful clergyman called Bob Wickham who was the headmaster of a rather chic preparatory school on the other side of the lane on which we lived, appeared in a state of some agitation. He said that the elderly spinster who looked after the youngest class in the school had been taken to hospital with a fallen womb. Could I possibly stand in for her for a while? I was unlikely to be brought down with the same complaint. I happily agreed and next day confronted my minute charges. Some of them were just literate and I set them to some writing task or other while I read Wordsworth's *Rainbow* and other suitable poems to the remainder. After this had gone on for some time a delightful slender boy from the writing group came up to me bringing his exercise book and asked for some assistance. As I was giving it, the light of comprehension seemed to drive a sense of where he was from his mind and he put his arm round my neck and said, "But Mummy, what do I do next?" I felt I must be destined for a career in teaching.

After a few weeks of this delightful work I was required to report to RAF Membury, somewhere in the Berkshire Downs. There were Stan and Wally and the wireless operator, but the more martial part of the crew had been removed. Our job at Membury was principally to run a kind of aerial pony express service

between England and the British zone of Germany. We had a regular bus route: first stop, Minden; next stop Bückerburg airport,
Hamburg. We took mail, invalids and others in need of rapid tran-
sit over the North Sea. I was always deeply moved as we left behind
the steeply pitched roofs of Germany and Holland to see coming
up before us the lovely domestic architecture of rural Norfolk.
Once in a while we got to stay over for the night in Hamburg
where we put up in some luxury at the Atlantic Hotel. I often
hoped we might wangle a longer stay than overnight until I heard
the story of another crew from our station, one of whose engines
had simply fallen out of the plane while they were flying near The
Hague. We were flying Dakotas at this time, phased out by the
Americans once their airframes had done 2,000 hours. But such
splendid planes were they that the pilot got it down at what was
then a very small airport at The Hague. It was impossible to get the
engine put back in short order and they had two glorious weeks in
Holland. A court of inquiry found that all but 3 of the 18 bolts
holding the engine into position had sheared off which cast an
unfavourable light on post war standards of maintenance.

Another of our tasks was to take up recently repaired aircraft and fly them about a bit to see that they were all right. In dis-
charging this duty we could go where we liked and we chose to
go to fly around Twyford, which was not too far away. Stan would
take the Dakota down as far as he could without courting trouble.
My mother would then emerge on to the lawn and wave at us
apparently in heartfelt greetings, and Stan would rock the plane
from side to side in a return greeting. A little later I found that she
was not applauding our appearance but trying to get us to go away.
As our last job, the day before we were demobbed, when we
thought that everything was over, we were sent up to find out what

had happened to a Gloster Meteor, one of the first – perhaps the first of jet fighters. It had taken off on a test flight and contact had been lost. We floated around the countryside between Membury and Bristol and before long came upon the melancholy relics of the crashed Meteor. It looked like a large snail that somebody's boot had squashed and dragged along.

The next day, 4th October 1946, I was demobilised. I went to Uxbridge and was efficiently equipped with a very flashy bright blue pin-striped suit, a dark brown trilby and a pair of rather yellow shoes. There was also an overcoat and a quite impossible tie. Dressed in my full finery of suit, hat and shoes, the best possible interpretation that could be put on me was that I was an experienced receiver of stolen goods. To prevent this impression getting about, I tended to wear the three items separately. I had only a week at home.

CHAPTER SIX
BACK TO OXFORD

Oxford

On the 11th I headed back for Oxford. No more beautiful mini-suite in Peckwater Quad, but a set in Meadow Buildings, up a narrow staircase. The roof was immediately above me and in the hard winter that followed, some water leaked through it on to my bed and froze hard on the eiderdown. I called round on the Steward (i.e. Domestic Bursar) and asked him if there was any possibility of someone coming to plug the leak. Even in the rough and tumble life of the period immediately after the war, he was surprised by my extreme mildness.

I had decided – and I still wonder whether rightly or wrongly – to abandon history and to read philosophy, politics and economics. I had already acquired quite a lively interest in philosophy. I had taken out C.E.M. Joad's really rather admirable *Guide to Philosophy* from the Stowe library and had gone on to read some of his other books. I had been given a copy of Bertrand Russell's *History of Western Philosophy*, which had just come out by my aunt Laura, the rather glamorous and somewhat disapproved-of wife of my mother's elder brother Tom. It was a fateful gift. I took to the subject with garrulous enthusiasm. My main tutor was Jim Urmson who had won an M.C. and been a prisoner-of-war in North Africa. He was extremely kind and attentive and had the great merit of not being too ferociously clever. He looked a little like Norman Wisdom, but better turned out. He was a loyal but not absolutely rigid disciple of the leading Oxford philosopher of the moment, J.L. Austin. My other main philosophy tutor was Michael Foster, a rather tormented figure who eventually committed suicide. It was not my fault. I think he found it impossible to reconcile his honest commitment to philosophy with an active and literal religious faith. That has not caused a number of other philosophers professing religious commitments from breezing smoothly through the tangles that carried him away. Politics was in the hands of the always delightful Robert Blake, and economics largely dispensed by the distinguished, but by then worn-out Roy Harrod. Tutorials with Harrod tended to concentrate on the sort of issues you would find discussed in the business pages of the newspapers and were principally interesting for the unremitting and usually unsuccessful efforts, which he made to keep his minute coal fire alight. I was also sent out, notably to two very good, very different philosophy tutors in St. John's. One of them, Paul Grice, spent most of the two and a half hour sessions in silence, but the fragments of conversation were excellent. John Mabbott had the odd habit of making notes as one read out one's essay, but it may have contributed to effective tuition. He wore a camel-hair coat that was quite worldly for a don in those days. Reflecting on his note-taking, I am not vain enough to suppose that he was doing what Hugh Trevor-Roper did to a friend of mine, John Cooper. The two of them held a seminar together on some such topic as the economic background of the English Civil War. Trevor-Roper would read a paper containing all sorts of wild generalisations and when John Cooper opened the discussion he would bring out a notebook, write all Cooper's corrective data down and save himself a lot of work.

I loved the lectures of the much-admired J.L. Austin, which took place in the Hall at Magdalen College. It was vital to arrive early to get a decent seat. The lectures were delivered in a slow, very well articulated way, in the style of P.G. Wodehouse with many dry jokes and felicities of language. To explain why every complete thought or sentence required a subject or topic and a predicate or comment, he said, "It would be no use receiving a telegram saying 'look here, old man, am in an awful hole' without any indication of who sent it." Gilbert Ryle's lectures also combined intellectual instruction with aesthetic pleasure. They consisted almost entirely of a series of epigrams laden with homely analogies and metaphors. I went to the economics lectures of one somewhat prosy New College don, which had the considerable merit of being delivered to audiences to whose members a mimeographed summary had been distributed when they came into the room. I went to quite a few lectures outside my field, but on the whole these were years of hard work at what I was supposed to be working at. The reason for this is that I came back to Oxford expecting to take things up where I left them off in the summer of 1943, hoping for all sorts of chaotic pleasures and soon found there were none to be had. The place was filled with ageing ex-servicemen, often with wives and infants who were anxious to get a degree as soon as possible. These were hardly party material. Things began to pick up from the hedonistic point of view after a year or two, when they had worked their way through the system. But for me, the work habit had taken hold by then. Borys had left for London but he came to Oxford from time to time to liven things up and could frequently be visited in London. My first new friend in post-war Oxford, even if he finally went into the drink trade, Tom Jago, was about as dutiful as I was.

Now that the war was over, travel outside England was possible. In the summer of 1947 I was in charge of the arrangements for the Christ Church Commemoration Ball. Before it took place I was stuck in bed with jaundice and passed the evening there with dancers coming in for a while to have a chat and putting away more champagne than is ideally prescribed for sufferers from this complaint. Before falling ill I had arranged a fine tour with Jim Buckley and two other friends. This I duly took part in, rising from my bed of pain. My convalescent technique, self-prescribed, was to have a glass of Dubonnet every night before dinner. It worked perfectly and I am happy to express my gratitude. Our route was ambitious. We wanted to see as many as possible of the places it would be good to visit for a longer period in subsequent years as we could. We went down the west coast of France to Biarritz where one of our number nearly drowned after foolishly swimming out to the large rock that stands some considerable way out from the beach, and to St. Jean-de-Luz which I thought delightful and planned to revisit at the earliest opportunity. I have never been back there. We then turned east and explored the Pyrenees where an incident occurred calculated to make one proud to be British. After a morning of fairly precipitous hills our ancient Vauxhall was emitting steam in a grief-stricken way. We decided to give it a rest and made our way into a small, partly white-washed shed which showed signs of being a bar. Seated with our drinks, we saw a young man come in with an enormous red setter. As he headed for the bar he looked toward this fine beast and said "Siddown, Lucien."

Monte Carlo, Menton and then down the western coast of Italy to Pisa, then to Florence and then over to the Adriatic. And finally up to Venice. This first visit had a powerful effect on me. Ever since I have been able to go, I have gone there for some weeks nearly every year and I am not in the least tired of it although I have developed something of a sideline for Sicily in recent years, but that has not led to regular visits.

Returning to my college in October 1947, I moved to a much more agreeable set of rooms than my leaky Meadow Buildings garret: a one bedroom set on the north side of Peckwater quadrangle. Here I was only a few yards away from the wonderful college library. It had a lot of material upstairs which only ardent researchers cared to examine, the stacks, being all round a shiny floor which I thought would be a wonderful place for a dance. It would probably not have borne the weight. Here I found a volume of state trials that contained the pathetic tale of Mervyn, Lord Audley, who was beheaded for compelling his wife to copulate in his presence with a footman with whom he was having an affair.

The food in Hall exhibited patriotic bleakness. A regular main dish was *Pilaff Milanese*, which consisted of partially mashed potato that revealed, on inspection by our sharp young eyes, minute red fibres of meat. I said that although the Italians had recently been our enemy, to hold them responsible for this dish was carrying vengefulness too far. To make up for these deficiencies, several of us would set off along King Edward and Turl Streets for the good old Taj Mahal where the technique of appeasing the appetites of a hungry nation was part of their tradition. For some quaint reason dinner in Christ Church was held at 7.20. Two Etonian friends of Euan's – Colin Tennant and Edward Montagu – would come in hungry from their New College dinner, served at 7.00, to eat another austerity dinner free of charge. Nobody raised any questions about their presence.

At school I had been enchanted, possibly intoxicated, by Spengler's absurd and wonderful *The Decline of the West*. Now, at Oxford, I came upon the cure: Popper's *Open Society*. I was as much influenced by this book and others of his early writings as by anything else I read in philosophy. But, like every other nascent philosopher in the place, I laid A.J. Ayer's crystalline *Language, Truth and Logic* heavily under contribution and Gilbert Ryle's *Concept of Mind* as soon as it came out. I went to a number of philosophical societies. One of them was run by a leathery dyke called Stella Aldwinkle and dealt with problems relating philosophy to religion. One night I went to a paper by C.S. Lewis, arguing that determinism refuted itself because anyone who believed in it had been irresistibly caused to do so. Then, glowing with pleasure at this masterly piece of reasoning, he was terribly disconcerted when Elizabeth Anscombe, a formidable Wittgensteinian bruiser, quite rightly pointed out the correctness of my belief that there is a tulip in front of me is not in any way undermined by the fact that it is caused by somebody holding a tulip up in front of me. At another, more professional gathering, I saw Wittgenstein *in the flesh*. Miss Anscombe asked me to show him around Christ Church and its garden the next day. This I duly did and he was a very nice and enthusiastic sightseer. I say this since I have subsequently come to think of him as a quite deplorable figure as a person above all, and also as an intellectual influence. But his English diction was beyond reproach, unlike that of some of his Austrian compatriots. Popper, for instance, had a reasonably tolerable accent but would Teutonise word-order under the pressure of discussion. I remember hearing him say, "I refer, of course, to the now by Dr. Toulmin very wisely abandoned theory that..." The real word mangler was Friedrich Waismann, a personage of some pathos who had been toiling away at a book about Wittgenstein's philosophy, which he was constantly compelled by its hero to tear up and start again. One of his best expressions was "koesal lowss" (for causal laws) and "vuurds" (for words), the principal object of his investigations.

Culture, of course, was thick on the ground in Oxford, more than one could cope with if one was going to do any academic work. The library was close by; the Ashmolean was not far off. There was so much music of every conceivable sort that one could easily become overwhelmed by it. I was choosy and just went to an occasional grand concert in the Sheldonian. Highly important was the cinema, above all that temple of pleasure: the Scala Cinema in Walton Street, a stylistic relative of the green corrugated iron cinema I had previously gone to in Winchester. Every now and then they had a Marx Brothers festival wrecking every afternoon for a week. It must have been at the Scala where the great incident occurred, in a showing of *Sanders of the River* when a primitive vessel floated into view with the noble figure of Paul Robeson at the helm egging on the dusky rowers evoking from the audience the cry of "Well rowed, Balliol!"

Another eventful journey I took must have taken place during the late summer of 1948. The man below me in my leaky garret in Meadow Buildings was a romantic, bearded, piratical figure (naturally the son of a professor of an obscure part of English literature). He was getting up a student party to visit Finland at the invitation of their students' union. I happily agreed, but when the time came, he was not of the party which had only three members: me, Charles Fisher – a son of the then Archbishop of Canterbury, and Geoff Dickens, a fellow of Keble and a leading expert on the Reformation. The night before we left from Tilbury we spent in Lambeth Palace. Charles's mother taught me a very useful recitation. It has to be pronounced with all the *ous* being given the full Edward Herath treatment (i.e. *aeou*): "I lounged downtown to scout around the council houses when out bounced Towser with a fowl in his mouth. Down Towser, down, I shouted and gave him a clout in the snout." From Tilbury we sailed in a Russian ship, the *Sestroretsk*, through the Kiel Canal to Copenhagen. Here Charles and I had a bit of a failure. We went into a restaurant and, believing *Smørrebrød* to be the chief national dish, passionately scrutinised the giant menu of the otherwise quite unassuming restaurant. The crucial word appeared nowhere. In one corner of the menu we found two special items: *Puk anretning* and *Luksus anretning* at 4.50 kr and 10 kr respectively. Not on the largest of budgets we opted for the former and a procession of charming girls brought dish after dish of sublime but still recognisably *hors d'oeuvre*-like items to our table. We set to and with enormous strength of will managed to consume nearly all of it, increasingly conscious of the looks of admiration on the waitresses' faces. They then, to our astonishment and discomfort, brought a series of substantial main dishes. (I remember a huge tureen of mince and another filled with chops wallowing about in gravy). We did our best, which became increasingly feeble amid rapidly decreasing respect from the waitresses. We concluded that '*anretning*' means 'set meal', but how were we to know?

Our next stop was Stockholm. On the dock as we approached were a number of what appeared to be homosexual prostitutes whose hair looked dyed and whose lips looked made-up. I conveyed this hypothesis to a fine Swedish journalist we had made friends with and he said that I was mistaken and that in fact they were Customs officials. This prepared me for what was to come. A Swedish girl we had made friends with asked us to a dinner party at her parents' house outside the city. This turned out to be the Swedish Sandhurst of which her father was commandant. Because she was so very lady-like, we had got ourselves in our best suits and had learnt that at Swedish dinner parties every male guest has to toast the hostess. She is expected to take very small sips in response to these courtesies. Perhaps the most striking thing in Stockholm was NK (Enko), the big department store of the city. Coming from the rather Mother Hubbard-like shops of England to this magical abundance was delightful. Among our fellow passengers was the Russian ambassador to Australia, returning home perhaps to be shot as a reward for his services. It was very pleasant to see the expressions of shock on his and his wife's faces as they contemplated the piteous failure of capitalism to accommodate the desires of those who lived under it.

In Finland there was quite a number of gently official occasions. One was the opening of the academic year at the University. We were given privileged seats in the front row. The Rector, a distinguished Latinist, spoke for three quarters of an hour in Finnish, which is hardly to be wondered at. Finnish is not a language that a speaker of ordinary Western languages can make a shot at interpreting if he has never studied it. Every word is accented on the first syllable. The main consonants in the middle of the words seem to be 'l' and 'm'. The result is something like this: "Himmele billeme pimmele." He then spoke for a quarter of an hour in Swedish. This had a rapid soporific effect on my two companions. Sensing this, I felt I must at all costs stay awake for the sake of Anglo-Finnish relations. Unfortunately a press photographer took a kind of panoramic photograph of the occasion, with the gowned Rector gesturing away on the podium and my comrades looking like drugged men-at-arms in some medieval legend while I sat straight upright between them with my eyes unnaturally wide open as if I were being electrocuted. This photograph was prominently displayed on the front page the next morning in the *Helsingin Sanomat* or whatever the main daily was called.

Drinking played a large part in our visit. There was a very humane practice followed in Helsinki by which hopelessly drunk working men were picked up in parks by the police after drawing their week's pay on Friday to buy spirit at the liquor store, for there were no straightforward bars for them to drink in. They were then allowed to sleep it off in the warm police station (*Pollisi Asema*) until they were sober enough the next morning to be sent home. At the yacht club we took part in a traditional sauna (a Finnish invention, after all). We sat naked in a log hut while water was poured by white-aproned old ladies over heated stones to produce the required steam heat. After several years' accumulation of bodily fluids had been extracted, we were supposed to jump into the Gulf of Bothnia outside. Charles complied immediately. I walked in a rather stately manner into the freezing water, gritting my teeth. Geoff Dickens found this too demanding and abandoned the swim after dipping his feet into the water and splashing a little of it over his chest, with the result that he got the most frightful cold. We had gone to the sauna with an excellent selection of girls but we were not, to our slight dismay, all naked together. In sophisticated

Helsinki, men and women were separated for sauna purposes. However, they were done to a turn before we were, so I hurried over to a large porthole in the wall to have a good look as they lollopped to the water. "You can see better from here," said Hannu, one of our Finnish friends, proving that Finns, despite their free and easy ways, were not all that blasé. Presumably dried out by this ordeal we had an enormous amount to drink before, during and after dinner. As we rolled home, the Domus Academica, an ultra-modern hall of residence in which we were lodged, loomed up before us, only one of its large windows lit up at this late hour. By its light could be seen two fine young women passionately grappling. A little stunned by this, we lurched to a halt to see how things would turn out. After quite a long pause, Erkki, a strong, blond wholesome lad observed "Boggers iss not wery common in Finland." Hannu, more a man of the world, muttered in my ear, "Lesspians, huh?" At the end of our stay they gave Charles and me a commemorative medal each, really for drinking. They compared our performance to that of a similar Swedish delegation that had had to be taken to the boat in an ambulance.

Back in Oxford for my final undergraduate year, I worked away. The final examinations were held in June. Each day for several days, I had to sit two three-hour papers. It seemed clear to me that this was going to be a considerable drain on one's stamina, so I resolved each day, on being released from the examination hall, to hasten up Broad Street to the Kemp Cafeteria for a gigantic tea. This did the trick. In due course it turned out that I had done quite well. At that time I had given up my earlier plan to be a barrister and had gradually replaced it with the idea of going into the Civil Service. For that I needed to do another exam, so I resolved to embark on some sort of graduate degree in Oxford. In the meantime I put myself in for the prize fellowship examination at All Souls. I finally left college after eleven terms residence in all and rented a small flat from two Catholic ladies in North Oxford. They lived with their brother, a retired schoolmaster, in the rest of the building that contained, as a tribute to their exceptional piety, a private chapel, into which I did not intrude. But I did attend with great pleasure the admirable teas they had on Sundays for the Catholic *jeunesse dorée* of the University.

CHAPTER SEVEN
ALL SOULS

The Codrington Library, All Souls

I arrived for the examination at All Souls with about twenty other aspirants, early in October. Among those present was a man with a loud, honking voice of whom I was not at all fond, called Richard Wollheim. He was accompanied by a young and glamorous fellow of Balliol called Marcus Dick. (The only professional philosopher I have ever heard of in Oxford who never published a single word, though some others ran him pretty close.) As we milled about waiting to be conducted to the hall, Marcus, casting a supercilious eye over our slightly tattered assembly, remarked "Not much competition here, Richard." I found this a real stimulus to doing as well as I could. And so it proved: three fellowships had been offered and I got the only one that was awarded that year.

A few weeks later, on a Saturday afternoon, I was about to set out in my utility 'sports jacket' for the shops of South Parade. Top of my list was sausages, to be cooked for our supper by a very nice girl who was later none-too-happily married to a gifted but pretty nasty Labour Cabinet Minister. An enormous American car drew up as I was about to leave and a cheerful man, whom I found to be an All Souls college servant, had come to announce the altogether enchanting fact of my election and also to take me down to the college to meet some of the Fellows. There they were in the front Quad, the Master of the Rolls (Wilfred Greene), the car's owner, that great Renaissance man, John Foster and a couple of others. I was bidden to come to dinner the following night (black tie) and to make arrangements to come into residence as soon as possible.

I duly came in, enjoyed the occasion, confiding to a person of my own age seated next to me at dessert, "This seems a nice cosy billet," which confidence the rotter put into wide circulation. But I could not get chucked out for that. Yet cosy it certainly was. I had a darkish room on the ground floor of the front Quad to start with, but moved quite soon into a much better set immediately above which had once been occupied by T.E. Lawrence (of Arabia). He had decorated the fireplace with some bits of medieval wallpaper, which I was very proud to point out to visitors. Breakfast went on in the morning in the Common Room until 10 a.m. Even so, when my friend from Christ Church, Michael Dummett, was elected the following year and had a room on the same staircase, it was my duty at ten to 10 to go and shake him into consciousness so that he did not miss breakfast. I met a number of splendid people in All Souls, just a bit older than me: Raymond Carr, John Cooper and Ian Little. Raymond, from humble beginnings in

Dorset had acquired the manner and tastes of a twentieth century Lord Rochester. John Cooper, also a historian, was of a starkly opposite nature. I always thought of him as a human Eeyore, slow speaking and given to banging himself on the back of his head while the conversation oozed out. I remember the opening sentence of a lecture he gave: "The first volume of Sir Winston Churchill's *History of the Second World War* reflects the gravest discredit on the historical jam-making factory responsible for its production." (A cruel swipe at F.W. Deakin and others who did most of the work for the great man to Churchillise stylistically.) Ian Little, a very handsome man, was also very pale. I put this down to a wartime job he had, testing prototype aircraft with a view to having them brought into general wartime use. These were often pretty speculative contraptions that only the greatest flying skill could bring to the ground in approximately one piece. He had approached All Souls by an unusual route. After demobilisation he hung around bridge clubs in London (the Portland and others) with a view to becoming a bridge professional himself. He was persuaded by an old schoolfriend – Monty Woodhouse – that he should take up a place offered him at Oxford, despite the fact that he had done no work at school. His powerful native intelligence got him through his first hurdle successfully and he then tried for All Souls. Here he was elected on the basis of his brilliant economics papers, the more generalised remainder being taken more or less on trust.

There were three main groups in the college: first, the Senior Fellows, important public figures like Lord Simon, L.S. Amery, Lord Brand and their like; secondly the professoriate, distinguished men at the height of their careers assigned to All Souls to provide them with an academic home who were mainly to be seen at lunch, tea and college meetings, and thirdly the Prize Fellows, youths like myself with an average age in their mid-twenties. As a result the weekends were highly sociable with large numbers in for all meals and particularly so when an important college meeting was scheduled for the Saturday. The second and third groups made weekday lunches quite popular but at weekday, breakfast and dinner numbers were much smaller. It was at breakfast that the appalling A.L. Rowse came into his own. He was vain, aggressive and paranoid, all to a very pronounced degree. He was not altogether a bad-looking man if you could distract your attention from his gigantic bottom. His conversational technique at breakfast was to make a generally abusive remark to some crony or catspaw while looking at, and clearly intending to refer to, someone else at the table. "Some people seems to think, don't they Norman or David that if you give a few feeble talks on the Third Programme and don't publish anything, you have done your duty by the college," all the while staring fixedly at some Prize Fellow. There were some nice men among the professors, for example Professor Jolowicz, who was always leaving the Fellows' lavatory just as I was arriving at it (or vice versa). The only reasonable explanation for this astonishing coincidence, since at that age I went there only twice a day, was that he was there nearly all the time. There was the dreadfully emotional but kindly Harold Hanbury who was distracted on Guy Fawkes Night by the distress he supposed to be caused by the fireworks to domestic animals in their neighbourhood. There was Sarvepali Radhakrishnan who was gifted enough to combine the offices (and stipends) of Indian Ambassador to Moscow, Vice-Chancellor of the University of Benares and Spalding Professor of Eastern Religions and Ethics. When in residence, which was admittedly not that often, he preserved his integrity as an Indian Holy Man by always bathing in running water. This Hindu quirk had two effects: it emptied the boiler of hot water for a considerable time and secondly infuriated all the other people on the same staircase, hoping for a bath. One night when he was presiding in Common Room, Michael Dummett and I were anxious to get to the meeting of some philosophical society. Being a non-drinker he did not detain us for long. As we took a quick cup of coffee, this sacred man turned to us with a conspiratorial smile and said "Are you young men going out on the town then?" an enquiry calculated to arouse Bollywood images of oriental lubricity.

I settled down to what I now intended to be a dissertation for the D.Phil in place of the lesser graduate qualification I had embarked on at the beginning of my graduate life. A large, genial classicist who had left the college recently for a tutorial post in another college, told me it was far too *infra dig* (as he put it, speaking as a classicist no doubt) for a Fellow of All Souls to work for a D.Phil, flying in the face of quite a bit of precedent. But I was quite happy to be guided away into a great deal of sorely needed miscellaneous study. It was as if I had been set free in Harrods in one department after another and not confined rigidly to underwear or health requisites. He himself was a possible object of the specimen Rowse remark a little while ago since it was not until the mid 1970s that he was able to conquer the fastidiousness that had prevented him from exposing himself to the ordeal of publication (to adopt a good old Oxford joke).

In the spring of 1951 I took up an invitation from the philosophy department at the University College of the Gold Coast (as Ghana was then called) near Accra to spend a term there. A jolly Australian was in charge, if that is the right term, and since all the people teaching there I can remember were non-philosophers, perhaps he and I were the entire department. I used to teach in a small white cylindrical hut with a conical thatched roof between 6 and 9 in the morning and sometimes late in the afternoon, so as to avoid the outrageous heat of the middle part of the day. Another environmental oddity of the place was its sunsets. One day I was sitting on my verandah looking over a splendid panorama of fields and copses with a cooling drink in my hand, when the telephone rang inside my house. It was not a lengthy conversation, two or three minutes at the most, but when I got back to the verandah the sun had disappeared below the horizon and the whole place was enveloped in darkness. I had a very pleasant servant called Patrick Ikposo. He came to me as I was about to leave the Gold Coast with his 'pass book' for me to sign with some supportive comments. Idly looking through it, I found that a few years ago two children had been born to him, Jones Ikposo and Lawrence Ikposo. They had come into the world some days apart in the same year. I suggested that one of these young men must surely have been born in a different year from the other. He looked at me with the laborious patience of someone frequently asked an ignorant question and said: "two wives." I enjoyed the story that during the riots that accompanied the imprisonment, or perhaps release, of Kwame Nkrumah a year or so before, if you drove into town you would frequently see policemen nervously changing into tribal costume from their uniforms so as not to get involved in any trouble.

I had come back a bit early because the dear nervous Warden Sumner had died and All Souls was in the grip of election fever which would be too good to miss. The contest was marvellously dramatic. The civilised element in the college supported the candidature of Isaiah Berlin, recently returned to it as a Research

Fellow from a tutorial post at New College. Against him was put an extremely faint Foreign Office dignitary whom I had never heard of before, called Sir Eric Becket. He was in fact a stooge for Rowse. The two candidates were neck-and-neck and it was somehow resolved, possibly in the face of Isaiah Berlin's withdrawal, to elect a fragile but agreeable professor of economics of the most unimpeachable Bloomsbury connections: Sir Hubert Henderson. Shortly after this event he attended the Vice-Chancellor's annual garden party and had a severe stroke. He was then removed to the Acland Home in Banbury Road and lingered there for some weeks. For all his fragility he was able to resist the earnest entreaties of the Sub-Warden, A.L. Rowse, to make way for a more robust candidate. I think he did manage to resign before he died. So the battle was on again, this time with Rowse standing in person. His main opponent was John Sparrow, a clever, highly entertaining and rather disreputable barrister. I and several others did not want Rowse at any price but thought that the particular kind of confirmed bachelorhood that was about all Sparrow had in common with him was not quite right for the college. We pressed the claim of the excellent professor of government, Kenneth Wheare, a marvellously relaxed Australian of great good humour and great good sense. One delightful feature of the election was the arrival from his job in Moscow of Radhakrishnan. We were all having some coffee and a breather in the Hawksmoor Quadrangle. Coming up to Isaiah Berlin, he asked in a penetrating voice, "Which way shall I vote, Berlin?" Lionel Butler, a Prize Fellow a little senior to me and a good friend until his death a few years ago, was wildly in favour of Sparrow. He led us to believe, quite correctly I suspect, that if we ran Wheare as well, we would, by splitting the anti-Rowse vote, give him the advantage of a substantial plurality. This was not to be countenanced. We swung our votes behind Sparrow and he was duly elected. He did not turn out to be an ideal Warden but he was a very entertaining one and did no serious harm.

The excitement of these elections was not the only enlivening event of 1951. In the first place I was involved in two matrimonial near-misses which I only just got out of. The first was to a handsome, rather stately, impossibly well made-up girl. She was always perfectly turned out, heavily made up and with a fine hair-do. The reason for this in part is that she was the protégée of a lady in an elevated position in the cosmetics industry who saw that she was given the best. It was all perfectly pleasant but unexciting and did not bode well for the long haul. We drifted apart quite pain-lessly. There was next a non-matrimonial interval: a fling with the wife of a philosopher in another college, more or less a nympho-maniac, which was no credit to my powers of persuasion. Nevertheless, the whole undertaking was extraordinarily pleasant. All that she wanted from me I was only too happy to give. Then I met a very nice girl from the North of England, of a county fam-ily. She was blonde, had a charming face – some might say her nose was too commanding, but I thought the world of it – but slightly imperfect legs. I was getting more and more entangled with her and I felt we could never be happy together. She had cultural long-ings but I think liked horses even more. So I did something which makes me cringe with shame fifty-five years later: I wrote her a pompous letter listing the respects in which we did not fit, proba-bly making it into a catalogue of what I supposed were her defi-ciencies. I am glad to say that she went on, in due course, to marry an extremely nice and astoundingly handsome man.

Shortly after the election of Warden Sparrow, I went to London to attend two weddings. One of them was that of Keith

Joseph, a somewhat older Fellow of All Souls, a very sweet man who went on to become Margaret Thatcher's Secretary for Trade and Industry. The other was that of Marcus Dick whose remark at the outset of my All Souls election exam had proved such a valuable incentive. I could get only to the reception for Keith's wedding at some grand London hotel. I arrived there to find a large throng of people talking at the tops of their voices. But this could not altogether distract me from the unusual sight of Isaiah Berlin in a top hat. I greeted a few people and then my eye fell on an altogether enchanting figure in the most delightful navy blue garment – a coat-dress is, I think, the technical term. I had for some time realised that weddings were ideal places at which to pick up girls: you do not have to be introduced and, on the other hand, if they wish to repel your advances they will not swing their handbags at you. Anyway, I was getting on quite well with this lovely person and had found out one or two vital facts: she was here from New York to attend a Shakespeare summer school and was at Keith's wedding to support the bride and whose sister, Ruth, was my enchantress's mother's secretary. She had very few guests on her side. All was going well until I noticed a number of friends circling round like wolves at the edge of an Indian encampment, who might be intending to get her away from me. So I decided to take her away, specifically to Marcus Dick's wedding at some other grand hotel. She was deeply shocked by this proposal, urging, in what I felt to be a rather straight-laced way for a New York girl of the 1950s that she could not possibly come since she had not been invited. The earnestness with which she expressed this old-fashioned reluctance led me to believe that she was not just brushing me off but really meant it. So I pressed ahead and soon we were on our way. As we left the second reception I invited her to come for a visit to Oxford – an essential complement for the transatlantic visitor to a stay in Stratford. She seemed rather anxious that I should not come all the way to her hotel, which was in a street just behind Marble Arch. I brushed this aside and the small hotel looked perfectly all right. (She had formed the view that it was a house of ill fame.) The Oxford visit was scheduled for some days ahead since I was leaving that night for Scotland to attend a conference of philosophers.

On the day of her visit I was in a poor condition. I had been at a party the night before in London where I had had a row with my second matrimonial near-miss and, dressed in a dinner jacket, I had caught a late train back to Oxford. Emotion and liquor combined to send me to sleep and when I woke up I was far beyond Oxford in Leamington Spa, the time being about 1 a.m. I asked a porter when the next train to Oxford was, hoping that I would not have to wait much more than half an hour, and he said the next train for Oxford was at 6.30 a.m. I went into the waiting room where there was no fire although it was a chilly night. I put this point to the porter who had given me the dire news about the next train to Oxford and he said, "Why, there ain't no fires after the end of May." I lay down on top of a large table in the middle of the waiting room and fell asleep. I was woken up by a brilliant light in my eyes which proved to come from the torch of a police sergeant. He was a most sympathetic man and after hearing my painful story, settled down for a cosy chat. He told me he had not always been a policeman but had, before joining the police, been foreman and sole male employee in a factory with 600 girls. "Well, as you can naturally imagine, I pretty soon had a nervous breakdown and went into the police for a calmer life." The train, stopping at every possible point, picked up at each of these halts, charming, fresh-faced, recently washed country girls coming to work in Oxford. I went to college and found I had left my keys with my day clothes in London, illustrating the principle that disasters tend to accumulate round one another. But was let in, pulled myself together and after a bit went to meet Marcelle's train.

I took her round selected sights. We had tea and dinner and then went to what I found to be a deeply engaging production of Milton's *Samson Agonistes* in the Hawksmoor Quadrangle of All Souls. The next day the same company was going to offer *Cymbeline* in the same Quad. But it turned out that I had to go to this on my own. Making some excuse, which once again I refused to accept as a brush-off, Marcelle returned to Stratford, urging me to visit her there some time the following week. Only later did I discover that she was dying of cold beside me at *Samson Agonistes* and did not dare to expose herself to an even longer process of refrigeration by staying for *Cymbeline*. I went to Stratford and we began the visit with dinner at the Shakespeare Head Hotel. So far as I could see, it was an excellent dinner that in normal circumstances I should have wolfed rapidly down. But I could hardly eat a morsel. This amazing state of affairs could have only one explanation: I was in love for the first time and, as it happened, for the last. We decided to go for a week to Venice where we stayed at the modest but entirely satisfactory Hotel Svizzera e Splendido Corso. Conditions were favourable for profoundly reinforcing the powerful impression that Venice had made on me during my motor trip four years before. I have never left so long an interval happen between visits to Venice since.

While we were there I asked Marcelle to marry me and she said she would, although there would probably be trouble with her parents because I was not Jewish. It was made clear to me that the marriage could not take place until she had completed her fourth year at her college, Bryn Mawr. Romantic passion warred in my bosom with respect for the academic propriety of her decision.

During the year of waiting I made one visit to the United States. I went down to Bryn Mawr where I was met by Marcelle with a tragic expression on her face. "This is a bad day for you to come," she said, "It's cold cuts on a Wednesday." In the dining room of her hall of residence I was the only man in a collection of about forty young ladies. I did not mind that. Nor did I mind the cold cuts, which proved to be wonderfully generous helpings of various kinds of cold meat. In New York I met her father for a rather chilly conversation, not at all like our conversations turned out to be after the deed was done.

I went down to pick Marcelle up in Southampton where she had arrived soon after the end of her term. We drove north to Oxford and stopped en route for lunch in a brick road-house. My appetite had come back, but it did not drive out my devotion. My All Souls friends were a great strength. Marcelle stayed with Ian Little and his wife on the River Thames for a while, he and John Cooper were the witnesses at our gloriously furtive little wedding in the St. Giles Register Office. Raymond Carr took us on as tenants on the top floor of his fairly spacious mansion in Great Milton where we stayed for two years until we bought a house of our own. We were very happy there and have been ever since.

ACKNOWLEDGMENTS

We would like to thank Jane, for having the idea for this book in the first place, Judy Moony for preparing a usable typescript, Grace for reading and correcting the manuscript, Brian McGuinness for his scrupulous proofreading, Joanna for her altogether magnificent work in bringing this book into publishable form with such imagintion and pertinacity and at the cost of a great deal of time and effort, and to Joanna Rose for her generous support and encouragement.